AMERICA'S BANKRUPTCY APPROACHES

HOW TO RESOLVE THE ISSUE AND PREVENT IT FROM REOCCURRING

AMERICA'S BANKRUPTCY APPROACHES

HOW TO RESOLVE THE ISSUE AND PREVENT IT FROM REOCCURRING

ARCHIE RICHARDS

DEFIANCE PRESS
& PUBLISHING

America's Bankruptcy Approaches

Printed in the United States of America

10 9 8 7 6 5 4 3 2 1

DEFIANCE PRESS
& PUBLISHING

ISBN-13: 978-1-948035-88-0 (Paperback)
ISBN-13: 978-1-948035-98-9 (ebook)

Published by Defiance Press and Publishing, LLC

Bulk orders of this book may be obtained by contacting Defiance Press and Publishing, LLC at: www.defiancepress.com.

Public Relations Dept. – Defiance Press & Publishing, LLC
281-581-9300
pr@defiancepress.com

Defiance Press & Publishing, LLC
281-581-9300
info@defiancepress.com

DEDICATION

I DEDICATE THIS BOOK TO my stepchildren, Tod, Sarah, Melissa, and Mariel. They were ages 7-to-17 when I entered their lives 48 years ago and married their Mom, who, unfortunately, has passed away. They are staunch liberals, but I admire them anyway. We just don't talk politics.

Acknowledgments

My Australian friend, Jim Foran, a wonderful writer, provided helpful advice for this book.

American friends, Jim and Barbara Walker, furnished encouragement throughout.

I am grateful to both.

TABLE OF CONTENTS

FOREWORD

SOME SECTIONS OF THIS BOOK were emailed to friends. Some of the shorter ones were printed as letters by the Concord Monitor. All such columns are archived in archierichards.blogspot.com.

Most source information not identified in footnotes came from what I considered to be creditable sources on the Web.

CHAPTER 1
Federal Bankruptcy Nears

RIDDLED WITH DEBT

WHAT COMES AFTER TRILLION?

Quadrillion. A single quadrillion is 1 followed by 12 zeros: 1,000,000,000,000.

After that comes quintillion: 1 followed by 15 zeros: 1,000,000,000,000,000.

A website of the Federal Reserve Bank of St. Louis, *All Sectors, Debt Securities and Loans,* reveals that the amount of debt at all levels in the United States is $81.8 quintillion.

That's 81,800,000,000,000,000—50 times higher than 50 years ago.

The U.S. population is 328 million (328,000,000).

Knocking off six zeros from each number leaves 81.8 billion divided by a measly 328. The total of U.S. debt securities and loans is thus $249 million per person—quite a burden we're carrying on our broad shoulders.

Well, not really. We are not each responsible for paying off all those loans. But indirectly, widespread debt does affect us all.

What on earth enabled such an incredible build-up of debt, especially the national debt?

Here's one reason, a darn good one, too, since it's been around for almost 90 years: The Federal Deposit Insurance Corporation

(FDIC) was created in 1933 to insure the security of individual bank accounts. This enabled bank depositors to avoid worrying about the safety of their deposits. If your bank makes faulty investments, the federal government foots the bill up to a hefty maximum. Only the rate of interest and the account's convenience need to concern you.

But a funny thing happened on the way to everlasting security. The federal government is close to bankruptcy. Late in the game, we're forced to worry about the security of our bank deposits after all, since banks hold trillions of dollars of federal debt. If the government stopped paying on those securities, the values of bank deposits would plummet.

All guarantees by the federal government are a mistake. Without the FDIC, people might have found ways to assure themselves that the loans being made by their banks were likely to be repaid. The level of debt might not have reached such astronomic levels.

The National Debt

At the end of George W. Bush's administration, the national debt was $10 trillion. The debt doubled during his administration. No spending piker was he.

The financial debt crisis hit in 2008, precipitating the long-lasting Great Recession. The crisis and recession were caused by eight federal policies. An explanation of these policies, taken from my earlier book, *America's Governments, Enemies of the Poor,* is reprinted nearby. Without them, the serious 2008 downturn would not have occurred.

The 2008 Credit Crisis Was Caused by Government

March 26, 2018. We're approaching the tenth anniversary of the 2008 Credit Crisis, which brought years of financial havoc. The Dow fell 54%. The unemployment rate more than doubled to 10%. It's true that banks and financial companies lowered their ethical standards, but this was induced by government requirements. The primary causes of the downturn were the following federal policies:

Since 1933, the Federal Deposit Insurance Corporation has insured bank deposits. All deposit guarantees are a mistake. They induce depositors to care about a bank's interest rate and convenience, but not the money's safety. The guarantees enabled debt to expand for decades throughout the economy. Without them, big depositors would have insisted on the safety of their money, reducing the nation's level of debt.

Beginning in the late-1990s, the Federal Reserve Bank expanded the money supply and lowered interest rates to excess. Increasing government regulations discouraged business investments. People bought real estate instead, and real estate prices soared.

In 2004, the Securities and Exchange Commission authorized five banks to accumulate unlimited debt. Previously, all banks had been required to restrict their debts to twelve times their assets. But Merrill Lynch, Lehman Brothers, and Bear Stearns, with their borrowings unlimited, all failed, their debts having risen up to forty times their assets.

By 2005, the Community Reinvestment Act had forced banks to lend at least 52% of their available mortgage money to people with low income. Regulators threatened to put banks that didn't comply out of business, and the regulators were deadly serious about it. To meet the requirement, banks had to make frenetic efforts to find sufficient numbers of low-income borrowers and therefore had to disregard potentially fraudulent loan applications. Ethical standards do not change quickly without provocation. The government's outrageous 52% requirement was just such a provocation. It forced banks to lower their underwriting standards.

Fannie Mae and Freddie Mac were sponsored by the government to bundle groups of mortgages and sell them as mortgage bonds to investors. This allowed loan originators to sell older loans and reinvest by offering new ones. In the early 2000s, the government also authorized higher-risk loans and urged companies to make such loans. The number of mortgages soared. Enormous profits ensued, especially since Fannie Mae and Freddie Mac had low borrowing costs due to widespread assumptions that the government would guarantee their loans. Other banks, with higher borrowing costs, competed by increasing the risks of their mortgage loans and securities. Large congressional campaign contributions helped the industry grow in size and risk. It would have been safer if an unlimited number of mortgage bundlers had competed with one another with no government involvement.

Standard & Poor's, Moody's, and Fitch were authorized by the government as the nation's principal evaluators of bonds. The government's earnestness about expanding home ownership and the widespread expectation that real estate prices would rise induced the three agencies to rate many mortgage bonds, including subprimes, with the highest triple-A rating. Again, it would have been safer if an unlimited number of bond evaluators had competed with one another with no government involvement.

The Mark-to-Market Rule, part of the Sarbanes-Oxley Act, required banks to value their mortgage loans and other assets for what they could be sold for almost immediately. It was as if your house had to be sold by day's end. After the credit crisis hit in 2008, the mortgage assets held by banks traded hardly at all, making reasonable valuations impossible. Banks had to lower their asset values way down, reducing lending substantially. The Mark-to-Market Rule was repealed in April of 2009, but not before it had done great damage.

After the 2008 bankruptcy of Lehman Brothers, the Federal Reserve required banks to raise their capital from 4% of assets to 7%. With the credit crisis having already begun, banks couldn't raise capital in public markets. They had to reduce their loan assets instead. During the next two years, commercial bank loans fell by 25%, the largest such reduction since the Great Depression.

These eight federal policies caused the 2008 credit crisis and the economic travails that followed. As with all serious economic downturns, the people hurt most were the poor.

But the downturn did occur. Because of it, the national debt between 2008 and 2016 ballooned from $10 trillion to $19 trillion.

Now, as of March 1, 2021, the national debt is $28 trillion. This is 134% of the U.S. Gross Domestic Product (GDP), that being the annual U.S. economic output. The debt is 7.7 times the annual federal revenues and larger than the GDPs of China, Japan, Germany, and India combined. In addition, President Biden has signed the $1.9 trillion Covid Relief Bill, most of which is not for Covid relief, but for unions and other constituencies of the Democratic left. Most of the cost will add to the national debt. The freebies included in this bill are so generous that literally millions of people will be paid more by not working than by returning to work, potentially reducing employment by five to seven million people.[1]

Over the past 12 years, while the national income grew only 30%, the national debt grew by 400%. We might be able to pay off the debt in a few years if we don't eat.

Okay, that won't work. How we can *really* pay off the national debt is proposed later in this chapter. But first, just how realistic is the threat of bankruptcy?

---

1. WSJ, Casey B. Milligan and Stephen Moore, *How Many Jobs Will the 'Stimulus' Kill?* 2/26/21.

Dear Reader, Economics may not be complicated to you, but it is to me. I try to write about it in a conversational style so simple and clear that even I understand it. —Archie

AMERICA IS CLOSER TO BANKRUPTCY THAN MOST PEOPLE KNOW

April 6, 2021

The national debt doesn't matter. We owe it to ourselves, right?

But "we ourselves" are adding to it as fast as we can. Perhaps you mean that *future* Americans will pay off the national debt.

Do you suppose we will have solved all of America's problems with deficit spending, making life cheery and prosperous for those future Americans, making them amenable to repaying our debts?

Dream on. The deficit spending will make the future all the more difficult. Future Americans will be even less likely to limit their consumption to repay our debts than we are to repay our own debts.

Some economists say it doesn't matter how high the national debt rises. Interest rates will remain at their current historic lows.

You better hope they're right. If interest rates do rise significantly, the payment of interest on the national debt would consume such a large portion of federal expenses that the nation would be forced to stop paying its debts.

Relevant Features of Money

The bills and coins we carry in our pockets, which are minted by the U.S. Treasury, are only just 3% of the nation's money. Most of our money consists of electronic numbers in bank accounts. The Federal Reserve Bank creates bank money out of nothing by pressing keys on a computer. It's easy as pie, and the Fed does a lot of it.

Say you buy a hamburger costing $5. Later on, after the amount of money has doubled because the swashbuckling Fed created so much of it, the hamburger would cost $10. That's inflation. To be more exact, if the number of dollars in circulation doubles in relation to the number of things and services available to buy, prices would double, and each dollar would have only half the buying power of the dollars held before. The deterioration of buying power of each dollar is especially hard on the elderly, who depend on their savings.

Under Federal Reserve management, the value of the dollar has indeed fallen. An item costing one dollar in 1913, when the Fed was created, would cost $26 today. The rate of that inflation was 3.1% a year in 108 years. (President Woodrow Wilson considered the creation of the Federal Reserve Bank his greatest accomplishment.)

Relevant Factors Determining Rates of Interest

When the Fed creates a great deal of money, dollars are in surplus. A surplus of anything causes its price to be low. (The price of money is the rate of interest when the money is lent.) Up to a point, the more money in circulation, the lower the interest rates.

Up to a point, that is. When creditors even begin to think that serious inflation is a possibility, they'll want higher interest rates to compensate for the loss of buying power.

In other words, a surplus of money at first causes interest rates to fall. Later, if creditors suspect that the buying power of their money may deteriorate, interest rates would then rise.

Debt Increases Economic Stress

Debt is implacable; it cannot be willed away. The interest cost each year crowds out other uses of the money. Higher and higher debt puts the economy under ever more stress. It makes the economy more precarious and economic changes more volatile. The element most volatile of all is likely to be interest rates.

The pace of growth of the national debt has increased. From 1800 to 2000, it grew at 5.7% a year. From 2000 to the present, it grew at 8.2% a year. Lately, the debt has increased faster than the Gross Domestic Product (GDP) and faster than most other federal expenses.

WHY AMERICA IS CLOSER TO BANKRUPTCY THAN MOST PEOPLE KNOW

The economy has been especially unsettling lately. The Credit Crisis occurred in 2008, following by the Great Recession, when the unemployment rate soared. Federal spending as a share of GDP surged to the highest level since World War II. The Federal Reserve created three trillion—yes, trillion—dollars, and interest rates fell.

The Credit Crunch was followed in 2020 by the Covid-19 lockdowns. Again, unemployment soared, and the Fed created more money to drive interest rates further down. The current interest rate of the bellwether Treasury bonds due in ten years is only 1.73%. With the volume of money greatly increased, the interest rate has declined.

But if the Fed creates too much money for too long, as it seems to be doing, inflation will result, pulling interest rates up instead of down.

The federal debt, as mentioned, is currently $28 trillion dollars. The interest paid on this debt amounts to $.345 trillion. Dividing this annual interest payment by the $28 trillion debt itself gives an interest rate of 1.23%. This is the low percentage interest the government currently pays on its debts.

The federal government's total annual *spending* amounts to $6.55 trillion. The $.345 trillion interest, divided by the $6.55 trillion expenses reveals that the portion of federal expenses devoted to the payment of interest is 5.27%. (Yes, the total spending includes the interest payments, but it makes me blurry-eyed to take this into account.)

Note that the portion of federal expenses required to pay interest on the debt (5.27%) is considerably higher than the rate of interest on the debt itself (1.23%). The reason for the disparity is the enormity of the debt.

"What if the rate rises?" you ask.

Good question. The Federal Reserve Bank expects interest rates to rise a little. But substantial increases? Naah, that can't happen.

Really? Substantial interest rate increases do indeed happen. The rate on 10-year Treasuries, as mentioned, is currently 1.73%. In March 2020, for reasons explained in Chapter 3 about Shadow Banking, the rate fell to 0.55%. Never in American history have the interest rates on 10-year Treasuries been anywhere near that low. Even the current rate of 1.73% is unusually low.

Here's a long-term chart of the interest rate on 10-year Treasury Bonds, which are considered the benchmark of all Treasury securities:

Note that, during the rampant inflation of 1981, the rate stood at 15%—far higher than the current 1.73%.

Currently, there are about $13 billion of the world's bonds whose rates are not just low; they're *negative*. Instead of creditors receiving interest from debtors, the creditors *pay* interest to the debtors for accepting and using the money. James Grant, of Grant's Interest Rate Observer, informs us that this has never happened before in 4,000 years of recorded interest rate history.

To avert financial disaster, much depends on the Federal Reserve Bank keeping interest rates at historic lows. Can the Fed accomplish this?

I doubt it. Throughout its history, the United States has undergone substantial economic swings, mostly caused, as discussed elsewhere in this book, by the government and/or the Federal Reserve Bank.

Following the Credit Crisis of 2008, high deficit spending induced the Federal Reserve to purchase substantial amounts of U.S. Treasury securities with newly created money. This is called "quantitative easing." High inflation did not result. The experts presume that continued quantitative easing will have the same beneficial effect.

Many experts have unchallenging faith in those who hold political power. If they're big government liberals, they gotta be reliable, right?

Such experts live in a dream world. Congress is adding to the debt like there's no tomorrow. Not just one, but *six* Covid-19 relief bills have been passed, including the recent $1.9 trillion blockbuster.[2]

The lockdowns may end because of the vaccines, in which case the economy is likely to pick up steam, raising interest rates. The Federal Reserve expects any such rise to be modest. It may eventually be more than modest.

In the last year, Congress has borrowed roughly $3.4 trillion to combat the economic fallout from the lockdowns. Adding the $1.9 trillion Relief Bill makes a total about equal to 25% of the GDP.[3] Additional risks emanate from Shadow Banking. The debt has made the economy precarious.

Mr. Biden is intent on expanding green energy projects. Sure,

2. WSJ, Mitt Romney, *Biden's Stimulus Bill is a $1.9 Trillion Clunker*, 2/23/21.
3. WSJ, Greg Ip, *The Era of Low Rates and Magical Thinking*, 1/30/21.

that'll save us all. The Heritage Foundation counts 25 green energy projects from the past. Each one has incurred multimillion-dollar tax-payer losses.[4]

80% of our energy comes from fossil fuels, only 3.7% from wind and solar.[5] Mr. Biden seems to want to upend that ratio. Given that fossil fuels are so much more efficient and reliable than wind and solar, the idea is preposterous. Germany invested big time in renewable energy. Whoops, Germany's utility bills have soared. The sun refuses to shine 24 cloudless hours a day, and the wind refuses to blow on demand.

Deficit spending already authorized represents 17% of the GDP. The recent income transfers to individuals and businesses will stimulate demand for years. President Biden's proposals would add another 9%. All of this is "magnitudes larger than President Obama's American Recovery and Reinvestment Act of 2009."[6]

After 2008, the trillions created for quantitative easing found their way into the reserves held by banks at the Federal Reserve. The Fed paid the banks interest high enough to induce the banks to retain the money at the Fed and not pass it out to the bank accounts of U.S. households, where it could have caused inflation. (Seems like over-activity to me, creating gobs of money with one hand and burying it with the other. But who am I to question my betters?)

In 2020, a tremendous amount of new stimulus money was passed out to U.S. households by the Treasury Department. Unlike in 2008, a considerable amount of this now sits in bank accounts, ready to be spent. Even before the recent distributions of $600 checks, personal savings were an estimated $1.5 trillion higher than pre-lockdown levels. The widespread administration of vaccines may unleash these

---

4. Washington Examiner, Stephen Moore, *Get Ready for More Obama-era Green Energy Scams*, 1/19/21.
5. Washington Examiner, Stephen Moore, *Biden wants to kill 80% of US Energy*, 2/2/21.
6. WSJ, Michael D. Bordo and Mickey D. Levy, *The Short March Back to Inflation*, 2/4/21.

funds, causing a potential wave of spending. According to the Fed, U.S. households held $2.2 trillion more in cash and cash equivalents at the end of the third quarter of 2020 than at the end of 2019.[7]

Meanwhile, Mr. Biden is launching regulatory assaults on energy, finance, small businesses, and healthcare.

Higher demand and potentially lower supply are a recipe for higher prices and higher interest rates.

How about the money from previous quantitative easing already held in reserve at the Fed? Never fear. The Fed thinks it can keep that bottled up by paying higher interest rates to the banks to keep it there.

Wait a minute. Higher rates mean increasing danger that the payment of interest on the national debt will overwhelm the nation's capacity to pay it.

Perhaps the Fed can thread the needle, that is, pay the banks enough to induce them to retain the money in reserve, but not so high as to stress the Treasury Department's ability to cover the interest on the total debt.

We're talking about massive amounts of money here, all controlled by the nine poor little Federal Reserve Governors, who run the place. The more the Fed creates new money to drive down interest rates, the more it runs the risk of high inflation.

America's financial ship of state is sailing into heavy seas. With the dynamics becoming ever tighter, is there no chance that the ship will spring a leak?

Let's assume that the rate on 10-year Treasuries returns to 4.5%, which is about the average on these bonds that has prevailed since 1870. It last hit 4.5% just 13 years ago. For the 35 years from 1967 to 2002, the rate was consistently higher than 4.5%, even reaching 15%.

A rise of the interest rate on 10-year Treasuries would not mean that the interest *payments* on the entire national debt would rise at

7. WSJ, Justin Lahart, *Saving Now Likely Means Spending Later,* 2/27/21.

the same pace. Treasury debt has a wide range of maturities, ranging from four weeks to thirty years. As the securities come due, they're rolled over to new debt, when the interest rate can be reset. Interest payments on new, 4-week debt would rise in 4 weeks, of course. Securities that came due in one year when they were first issued would gain higher interest payments only after the year has passed and the debt is rolled over. People that recently bought new 30-year bonds would have to wait 30 years for the interest payments on those bonds to rise. But over 60% of the securities that make up the national debt have maturities of less than three years.

The point is, when the interest rate on 10-year bonds go up, the increase of interest payments on the entire debt lags behind.

Okay, if the rate on 10-year Treasuries rises to 4.5%, what portion of total federal expenses would be devoted to cover the interest on the debt? To determine this, I must make various assumptions, which may of course be wrong. If arithmetic doesn't give you chills of delight, lop over the next four paragraphs and skip to the answer: 40.6%.

Interest of 4.5% on 10-year Treasuries would be 2.6 times higher than the current 1.73%.

I previously divided the government's $.345 trillion interest payments by the government's total annual *spending* of $6.55 trillion, to determine 5.27% as the current portion of federal expenses devoted to the payment of interest. Increasing 5.27% by 2.6 times, as above, would make it 13.7%. This seems unreasonably high to me. To make the assumption more conservative, I split the difference between 5.27% and 13.7%, making the assumed rate 9.5%.

Assume that the federal debt increases by 40% from the current $28 trillion to $39.2 trillion. After a lag, the interest rate on the entire national debt would then be 9.5%, as assumed in the last paragraph. The total interest *payments* for the year would be 9.5% of $39.2 trillion, or $3.72 trillion.

Further assume that total federal expenses have increased by 40% from the current $6.55 trillion to $9.17 trillion. Divide the $3.72 trillion assumed annual interest payments by the total assumed $9.17 trillion federal expenses for the year. The interest payment on the debt for the year would then constitute 40.6% of the year's expenses.

40.6%. Over forty percent of federal expenses would be needed just to cover the interest on the debt. The interest on *past* expenses would impinge significantly on current expenses. If the government has to borrow just to cover the interest payments, bankruptcy would be approaching like a freight train. The government would be so awash in debt that its nose would be at or possibly below the water line.

This dire result assumes that the interest rate on the 10-year Treasuries rises only to the average of the last 150 years. It could go higher. As you may see in the above chart, the rate was consistently over 6% for 21 years from 1972 to 1993.

Raise tax rates? It's likely that the government would already have raised the rates as high as possible. As discussed elsewhere in this book, the higher the rates, the weaker the economy, causing *less* government revenues, not more.

The European Central Bank and the Bank of Japan have also expanded their money supplies exponentially. Any significant increase of interest rates is likely to be worldwide.

The poor old Fed would have no room to rumble. Debt is an implacable foe. The higher it goes, the greater the economic volatility.

In bankruptcy, the Treasury would stop paying at least some of its debts, greatly reducing the value of the huge amounts of Treasury securities held throughout the economy. (Institutions bought so many trillions of federal securities because they were riskless, right?) America's wealth would be substantially reduced, hurting the poor most.

Alternatively, if the Fed generates runaway inflation, the national debt would be reduced to almost nothing. But all assets valued in dollars—bank accounts, insurance policies, bonds, Social Security, Medicare payments—would also be reduced to almost nothing. Widespread misery would prevail, again hurting the poor most.

Stopping payments of the debt would be horrific. Runaway inflation would be worse.

Many people support MAGA (Make America Great Again).

Too many people favor LARS (Let America Remain a Spendthrift).

PAPA seems appropriate: (Profligacy Makes American Poor Again).

Experts are prone to step aboard bandwagons. If they don't, and the bandwagon goes in the right direction, the experts would be left by the side of the road. But all too often, bandwagons go in the wrong direction. With today's heightened anxiety, I count four bandwagons: racism and diversity, excessive fear of Covid-19, opposition to Trump, and the belief that the national debt doesn't matter. All four, I maintain, will prove to be wrong.

Inflation could flair and interest rates could fly. We could eventually be over the cliff without a parachute. The American people, who remain productive, will be surprised, perplexed, and angry.

Is there a way out of this conundrum? Yes. Not an easy way, but the only realistic way, in the next section.

But first, a qualification:

Treasury Inflation-Protected Securities are referred to as TIPS. These are genuine U.S. Treasury securities. You can buy TIPS in units of $100, thereby becoming a creditor of the United States. They are issued with maturities of 5, 10, and 30 years. With these securities, the government, out of the kindness of its beating heart, protects you from the ravages of inflation, as measured by the Consumer Price Index (CPI).

TIPS differ from regular bonds as to the final payment of principal, when the bond matures and is paid off. With regular bonds, the final payment remains constant. With TIPS, the final payment is adjusted every six months. When the CPI shows the general price level to be rising, the final principal payment is raised. When the CPI shows the general price level to be falling, the final principal payment is reduced.

Currently, 5-year Treasuries and 5-year TIPS are priced so that the "breakeven rate" is 2.58%. This means that if annual inflation runs faster than 2.58% in the next five years, a person is better off buying TIPS. If inflation runs slower than 2.58%, one is better off with regular bonds.

The 10-year breakeven rate is lower: 2.35%. The 30-year breakeven rate is lower still: 2.08%.

All three of these breakeven rates are lower than the rates of inflation implied by the alarming scenario suggested by my analysis above. I see three possibilities:

The national debt continues to build. But the Federal Reserve Bank accomplishes a miracle and keeps interest rates low indefinitely, rendering bankruptcy unnecessary. A statue of Jerome Powell is erected in Washington, DC.

The current buyers of TIPS prove to be wrong. Inflation and interest rate both soar, and the United States declares bankruptcy.

Millions of copies of this book are sold, and the American people adopt its recommendations. Within five years, the national debt is largely paid off, and the government sector of the United States is greatly reduced. A statue of yours truly is erected in Washington, DC.

How to Pay the National Debt

The suggestions I make in this section you may not have thought of. You may not have heard anyone else express them. The problems they would cause are obvious and numerous. Therefore, the suggestions have got to be wrong.

If that's your reaction, I suggest you reread the last section and return here. I'll wait ...

Now, wouldn't you say that doing nothing about the U.S. national debt is a recipe for disaster? Wouldn't you agree that the debt must somehow be paid off, even though doing so will cause problems? Not doing so could be catastrophic.

A vital way the United States can at least reduce its debt is to exchange portions of the debt for things of value the government owns.

If you own a United States bond, you are a creditor of the U.S., and your bond is a U.S. liability. Let's say that something of value owned by the government passes into the hands of a corporation in exchange for the corporation accepting a portion of the nation's debt. The corporation would have the valuable item as an asset. It might also include your bond as a liability. You would then be a creditor of the corporation. You would probably be better off than you are now, because the United States government is close to being a deadbeat. If it goes under with you as a creditor, your bond would not be repaid.

Corporations create wealth, and they use some of the wealth to reduce their debts. Governments create no wealth and seldom pay down debt. In 1835, President Andrew Jackson paid off all of the nation's debt. In the 1980s, Margaret Thatcher paid off some of Great Britain's debt. But those are exceptions. Most governments continue to accumulate debt until they default. Some nations of South America are especially good at persuading rich folks to lend to them and defaulting again. Since 1816, Argentina has defaulted nine times.

When services such as the postal service are operated by government, they tend to run deficits. When those same services become owned by private parties, they tend to earn profits, which government can then tax, leaving the government better off than before.

Corporations and most private owners take into account the long-term prospects of the entities they own, including descendants and future shareholders. Government's time horizon extends mostly to the next election.

For private parties, competition and press publicity reduce waste and wrongdoing. Having no competition, government is permeated with waste and wrongdoing, a lot of it hidden. Elections are too infrequent and too far-removed to prevent these problems. A matrix of private ownership would preserve values and protect the environment far better than government.

Okay, down to business: The U.S. government owes $28 trillion. (I disregard the $6 trillion of additional debt owned by federal agencies.)

What does the government own that's of value?

Gold. The United States owns 261.5 million ounces of gold, currently priced at $1,752 an ounce, for a value of $4.6 trillion. That's a start. After it's sold, the government would have $23.4 trillion of debt to go ($28 trillion less $4.6 trillion).

Gold is not needed for monetary purposes. The monetary system recommended in this book is better than a gold-backed system. Gold is needed for the manufacture of warplanes and stuff, but industry can acquire gold for those purposes.

Land. The federal government owns roughly 640 million acres, an astounding 28% of the 2.27 billion acres of United States land.

The sale of 640 million acres of land would require a price of $36,600 an acre to pay off $23.4 trillion of government debt remaining after the sale of its gold. This of course is way unrealistic. But the government could nevertheless sell most of the land it owns to repay a portion of its debt. Land that's likely to generate profits in private hands should be sold first for the highest possible prices. Lands containing fossil fuels and other valuable minerals are likely to generate the most profits. The government should consider these potential values when offering its land for sale. Lands containing fossil fuels and other valuable minerals are likely to generate the most profits. The government should take into account these potential values when offering its land for sale.

As to U.S. land owned by the government in various states, Montana and Nevada come in first; the U.S. owns 85% of each. (These numbers are as of 2013.) Next comes Utah at 65%, Idaho at 63%, and Alaska at 61%. Alaska is so big that the U.S. owns more land there than in any other state.

"Alaska! Who would want to live among the mountains and far-away places of Alaska?"

Well, aren't people now signing up to move permanently to Mars, where they'll remain for life? The scenery there is barren, and if a person gets so much as a pinhole in his or her space suit, that's it, buddy, sayonara. From Alaska, at least you can vacation in Florida without a space suit.

Besides, you don't have to *live* in far-away Alaska. You'd probably have to own an airplane, but you can hike, cross-country ski, fish, hunt, and watch over your animals.

"What animals?"

"You'll be the owner of animals that cross your land."

"What! You mean the elk and other animals that happen to pass by? That's outrageous!"

"Sorry, the private ownership of animals is the best way to preserve them. 20,000 African elephants a year are estimated to be killed by poachers, especially for their valuable tusks. If the elephants could be privately owned by well-armed individuals, the poaching would come to a halt. The owners would charge tourists for viewing the animals and charge very high prices for hunters authorized to shoot them. In parts of Africa, elephants and lions are disappearing because no one owns them for profit. Passenger pigeons were once so numerous that their migrations clouded the skies. Since no one owned them, they became extinct. Alaskan elk are different, of course, but you get the idea. Private ownership generally enhances value; government ownership, which prevails now, does not."

National Parks

The national parks, which are of great value, should be auctioned off to the highest bidders.

"Come on! Sell the national parks? You gotta be kidding! Passing those breathtaking places into the hands of money-grubbing private parties? Our national treasures would be spoiled by enormous crowds and razzle-dazzle displays."

Think twice about that. The national parks cannot be duplicated. The U.S. should sell them for high prices. If the park owners allowed them to be spoiled by enormous crowds and razzle-dazzle displays, the parks would lose value. The loss of value would not be in the interest of the owners, aesthetically or financially.

"Aesthetically? Corporate managers aren't interested in aesthetics!"

They're finer people than you've been led to believe by the liberal media and television shows that often make a businessman the bad guy.

Corporations owning national parks would sell stock to the public. The public would not only be tourists, they would also be partial owners. Tourists would want the parks to maintain their breathtaking qualities. The shareholders would want the prices of their stocks to rise. Some people coming to see the national parks would be both tourists and shareholders.

The boards of directors of the corporations would weigh the conflicting interests and appoint managers capable of evaluating both on a daily basis. With a little change here and a little change there, such adjustments are more likely to be accomplished by private parties than by government.

The corporations would want the parks to be managed efficiently. Government is seldom efficient at anything (except perhaps for the development of vaccines with which former President Trump was heavily involved). Government's methods generally have the highest costs.

Government does not do well with conflicting goals on a daily basis. Eventually, such conflicts get up to Congress for resolution, but not until Congress gets around to it. When it finally decides, that's it, probably for years. In between, conflicting goals are dealt with by bureaucrats who have a predilection to exert force. They prefer not to delegate decisions to others, and they tend not to truly solve problems because this would make their jobs unnecessary. They also do whatever they can to avoid being blamed. Far better on all counts that matters be resolved daily by private managers on the ground.

Some current national parks, especially the recent ones, may be too large and too arid to serve profitably as tourist attractions. They could be sold for private use, mining, or whatever. They could charge hikers or bikers when it's profitable and not charge them when it's not. The new owners might be environmentalists who would simply hold the land without using it in any way. This would be fine too, as long as they paid up front to buy the land.

Private owners of national parks would be more adept than government at capturing and making the aesthetic experience of national parks available electronically, enabling millions of people, at least to some extent, to experience them. Private owners would also be adept in selling high-quality knowledge about geologic forces to schools for children to learn.

Nothing's perfect, of course, but private parties are more capable than government of negotiating between conflicting needs. The aesthetic grandeur of the national parks would be preserved, and more people than at present could experience them.

Here's the key: The United States must reduce its national debt. The national parks have high value. Their sale would help.

Other Land

The land directly under government office buildings would be retained. So would military bases, enabling the troops to sharpen their skills. The rest would go. Forests, rivers, mountains, parks, prairies, reservoirs, aquifers, swamps, deserts, tundra, dams, and inland waterways should all be sold to the highest bidders by all levels of the U.S. government.

Indian reservations, unfortunately, are replete with depression and alcoholism. From the very beginning, North American Indians should have been required to integrate with the rest of American culture. By now, 200 years later, the Indians would have been fully integrated by intermarriage, just as blacks and Hispanics are doing now.

The 52 million acres of Indian reservations should be sold to the highest bidders, some of whom might be North American Indians.

Radioactive land would sell cheap. Some volcanologists might be pleased to have their very own private volcano for intensive study.

Water

All sources of fresh water should be privately owned. Did California take advantage of heavy rains in recent years to build more reservoirs? Of course not. Recent California governments have been especially inept.

All rivers and inland waterways should be privately owned. Here's a quote from my previous book. I cannot say it better:

"If a corporation owned a portion of the Mississippi River, it could earn money from those who use the waters for transportation, irrigation, manufacturing, fishing, drinking, or recreation. If a river owner allows her portion of the Mississippi to become polluted, the downstream owner would sue. If the river's mouth is polluted, the owner of that portion of the Gulf of Mexico would sue. Monitoring pollution is cheaper than lawsuits, making lawsuits infrequent."

Given the many uses of its waters, the Mississippi River must be worth billions of dollars. The same for the Missouri, Hudson, and Columbia Rivers, Chesapeake Bay, aquifers and many other waters. The U.S. needs to realize these values to repay its debts.

The people who now use these various waters for free would complain about having to begin paying for them. Prices throughout the economy would have to adjust. But in the long run, society works best, with overall costs reduced, when all costs are known and accounted for. The environment benefits too. With government, costs are often swept under the rug and not accounted for.

Legislatures and the courts would have to work out to what extent the owner of a river would be liable when flood waters damage nearby homes and farms.

The United States claims ownership of 12 nautical miles off U.S. coasts. The ownership applies from the airspace above to the seabed below. There's oil in them thar seabeds, not to mention other valuable assets. Selling them would bring in substantial funds to reduce the federal debt.

No one would expect private parties to come up with cash to acquire these valuable properties. They would have to sell bonds or incur debts of some kind. But at the same time, the government's debt would be reduced. Initially, the level of debt would remain roughly the same, simply shifting from the government to the private sector.

But in the long run, private parties create wealth; government does not. Private parties reduce their debt; governments do not. Shifting the debt from public to private interests would be the nation's net gain.

In anticipation of these massive sales, do not assume that technologies will remain the same as they are today. In government, technologies and procedures tend to remain the same. In the private sector, technologies and procedures constantly improve. Things work better when the impact of government is reduced.

Forests

Onward and upward. Nationally owned forests should be sold. An unattended forest grows until it's choked with kindling. Charcoal deposits reveal that prehistoric wildfires destroyed more than 5 million acres every year, far more than fires have destroyed lately.

In the first half of the 20th Century, the federal government did a good job managing its forests. But in the 1970s, environmentalists pressured Congress to slow down the culling of trees. It's hard to know why. Perhaps they wanted people to return to nature. (Not the environmentalists themselves, of course; they're above that sort of thing.) Timber harvesting declined, and forest fires increased.

Forest fires flood the atmosphere with CO_2. Good forest management confines the carbon in living trees or in the wood from harvested trees.

Privately owned forests are culled to remove kindling and unwanted trees, with the result that the remaining trees don't burn. Pictures from the air of burnt government forests bordering on privately owned forests reveal a stark contrast. The government forest is black. The privately owned forest right next door is pristine green.

Congress is prone to be too specific in its directions (because it knows so much about everything, I suppose). Each year, it directs the Forest Service how many trees to cull. In past years, Congress demanded that an excess of trees be culled, resulting in the Forest Service engaging in clear-cutting. More recently, Congress has required that too few trees be culled, causing the danger of forest fires to grow. The Sierra, for example, can support about 80 mature trees in a typical acre. The current density is more than 300 trees.

I myself, hiking in the White Mountains of New Hampshire where forest fires have been suppressed for many years, have been distressed to see an excess of trees and an excess of kindling under the trees.

In both places, intense forest fires loom. Instead of blaming

Congress, as they should, the environmentalists will have a field day blaming global warming.

Private timber owners favor steady income and do not clear-cut their trees. They cull their forests to prevent a valuable asset from going up in smoke. Government has no profit, so it cares far less, except, of course, in its political speeches.

The national forests have enormous value, which is not being managed well by the government. The nation would be better off with their privatization.

Oh yes, and the U.S. must reduce its debts.

Transportation Facilities

Roads and bridges, including the interstates, should be sold to the highest bidders. Very likely, the new owners would eventually implant electronic devices in the roadways, and vehicle owners would be required to install corresponding electronics on the vehicles to use the road. An owner could then recognize the vehicle, its weight, the time of day, and maybe even the weather conditions. She would aggregate your various uses of the road and charge you accordingly. If you use a road during busy commuter hours, the charge should be higher. Some roads would probably be freebies.

Owners would establish the rules of the road and either hire or rent a police force. Overall, the cost of roads, no longer owned by government, would fall.

Heavy trucks are the main cause of road deterioration. With the roads owned by government, the trucking companies pay too little to cover the cost of repairs. The costs are instead added to tax bills. If the roads were sold to private parties, the truckers would be charged realistically for the repairs, and our taxes would fall.

Higher trucking costs would also reduce the number of trucks on the road, causing more goods to be carried by rail, especially on long trips, at which rail is so efficient. If the Jones Act is repealed (see Chapter 5), more goods would be carried by water, which is even more efficient, reducing costs all the more. The prices of goods thus carried would fall as well.

America's roads and bridges have great value. The government is unable to keep them in good condition without greatly increasing its national debt, which is unacceptable. Those facilities must be privatized to enable the government to reduce its debts.

The private owners of these lands and facilities could of course sell them to other private interests, but not return them to the government.

Urban Bus Transportation: The costs of government urban bus transportation are rising. But in most cities, ridership is falling. Buses emit more greenhouse gases per passenger mile than the average automobile. Buses nearly empty, which is all too often the case, do not relieve congestion; they add to it.

Urban transportation should be privatized as much as possible. People have smart phones and can call for a ride. A rider would not be robbed or abused if she has obvious possession of a weapon, knows how to use it, and the laws support her defensive use of it.

Amtrak carries about 87,000 passengers a year on 300 routes. It owns the trains and uses 21,400 miles of track that are mostly owned by private freight carriers. It loses money on 41 of its 44 routes and requires more than a billion dollars a year of support from the federal government to stay in business.

Congress insists that Amtrak offer routes that serve political purposes, even though the economics may be poor. The biggest losers are long-distance routes, such as New Orleans to Los Angeles. The quality of Amtrak's service is mediocre, and its trains are late about a quarter of the time. Some 20,000 employees earn an average of $105,000 a year in wages and benefits. Unions undermine efficiency by protecting poorly performing workers and insisting on inefficien-cies that require a larger staff. Privatization would reduce employee costs and close uneconomic routes.

Privatization of rail passenger service, a success in Great Britain, Japan, and Canada, should be undertaken in America. The government would knock a hole in its debt and reduce its expenditures.

Postal Service

It's crazy that the mailing cost is the same whether a letter is sent across the street or 7,900 miles as the crow flies from Baltimore, MD to Guam. Letters between Baltimore and Washington, DC would be less than $.55. Letters from a small town in Maryland to a small town in Idaho, or Guam, would be considerably more. This is as it should be. Prices should be set according to costs. Besides, technology is ren-dering many postal services obsolescent. Emails cost nothing. Postal deficits are growing. Covering them with taxes or piling them onto the federal deficit is outrageous.

The 630,000 people employed by the U.S. postal service are the world's highest-paid, semi-skilled workers. The service should be privatized. Selling the postal service would reduce America's costs, wipe out annual subsidies, and bring in cash up front.

I can't assure you that the privatization of the postal service would make the delivery of mail better or cheaper. Free markets in *health-care* would make healthcare better and cheaper, because free markets would unleash new medical technologies that have been suppressed by government intrusions. But a great deal of technology has already been developed in the delivery of information, a key reason why the postal service adds less value to American life than it did. Privatization would save federal costs—reason enough for the government to sell it.

All services provided by the government, including trash collec-tion, should be privatized.

I now consider valuable assets owned jointly with other nations:

The Oceans

Water covers 71% of the earth. 96.5% of it is salt water, 3.5% is fresh, over half in the form of ice. A substantial amount of fresh water also exists underground. (The world's largest aquifer is beneath the Sahara Desert.)

The oceans and seas offer tremendous value to mankind for transportation, fishing, recreation, and mining. Untold wealth exists in seabeds in the form of oil and many other materials. Oscillations of the ocean's surface could also be utilized to generate electricity.

Including South Sudan, which became independent in 2011, there are 196 independent nations on earth. Negotiating how much of the world's oceans should be owned by each nation would, of course, be a monumental task, especially since some nations, like Switzerland and Botswana, are land-locked. But everyone would benefit from the oceans being in private hands. As to the allocation of the value of the oceans among the nations, negotiators might bear in mind the following factors:

- The allocations might be larger for nations with bigger populations. This would benefit China, India, the USA, and Indonesia.

- The allocations might be larger for nations with larger Gross Domestic Products. This would benefit the USA, China, Japan, and Germany.

- The allocations might be larger for nations that have greater land mass. This would benefit Russia, Canada, the USA, China, Brazil, and Australia.

- The allocations might be larger for nations that are landlocked.

- The allocations might be smaller for nations that have larger national debts in relation to their GDP. This would disadvantage Japan, Greece, and possibly Italy, the USA and China. (There should be no reward for profligacy.)

- The allocations might be reduced for nations that are ruled by dictatorships. This would disadvantage North Korea, Argentina, Cuba, and China.

- The allocations might be reduced for nations that have hegemonic ambitions. This would reduce the allocations to China and, to a lesser extent, Russia.

Many of these suggested allocations would benefit China. Would this temper its hegemonic ambitions? I don't know. The wealthier and better educated the citizens of China become, the less likely they are to put up with dictatorship.

The oceans serve as a dump for the plastics and other detritus of mankind. One hopes that large ships with gaping maws are developed that can suck in large amounts of waste that ocean currents have accumulated in certain waters. If the ocean waters have not yet been privatized, all the world's nations should help pay for this clean-up. I expect technology will eventually be developed that can transform the molecules of waste into molecules of usable materials.

The more privatization of the world's resources, the safer the world becomes. Unlike governments, people have neither the inclination nor the money to initiate wars.

Other Features of Value

- Antarctica. The costs are high, but enormous value lies beneath that cold, snow-covered, and extraordinarily windy land.

- The Spectrum. Technology exists that can divide the spectrum into smaller and smaller distinct and useable segments.

How to Prevent Debt from Rebuilding

In the previous section, I suggested how to significantly reduce the national debt. Transferring things of value owned by government, such as gold, land, and the nation's transportation facilities to private parties would knock a substantial hole in the debt.

But with the things of value gone, it becomes essential that the debt not rebuild. Nothing would remain to exchange for the reduction of future accumulations. Government must therefore take on less and become significantly smaller. After the government backs off, people would learn to work things out themselves. The private sector in fact would flourish, with the poor helped most. (Government workers are not about to back off on their own. They would have to be forced to do so, ultimately by voters.)

With tax rates lower and responsibilities significantly reduced, the government could generate sufficient funds over time to pay off whatever portion of the debt not paid off previously.

Here's the basic problem: The United States Constitution set up a government that was responsive to the people's needs and desires. This was a big improvement over what had prevailed before, namely, government responsive to the needs of the elite. But accommodating the desires of the people has still proved, after two centuries, to generate enormous problems, especially the accumulation of debt.

The people want government to exercise force for good. But they are aware only of the immediate benefits of laws and regulations, which are obvious and often favorable. They are responsive to the names given to the bills by the legislatures, which of course are positive and laudatory. In the long term, however, the actual results of almost all government policies are neither obvious nor favorable. Most long-term results are opposite to the intended results.

Laws and regulations intended to do good may succeed in doing so in the short term. But in the long term, they unintentionally cause problems that far exceed the benefits apparent at the beginning. Many such problems are described in Chapter 5.

At about the time of the American Revolution, philosopher and economist Adam Smith pointed out that the hidden hand of free markets provides indirect and unintended benefits to society.

But the hidden hand of government brings indirect and unintended *harm* to society. As a general rule, voters do not know this. Neither do the people they elect.

Circumventing the U.S. Constitution isn't necessary. The best way to improve the quality of political leadership and make leaders more aware of the negative consequences of government's use of force is to do away with political professionalism.

Some protest that the complexity of modern life requires a large and intrusive government.

Hogwash! The people of America possess ever-greater expertise. If free markets were allowed to operate with minimal government intervention, the benefits of that expertise would permeate the entire nation, especially helping the poor.

U.S. Congress

U.S. House and Senate members should be limited to one term each, with much reduced pay. Two years for members of the House. Six years for senators. Get in, do the job, and get out. A Constitutional amendment might reduce the term for senators from six years to four.

Regardless of party, the longer people remain in Congress, the more they vote to increase the power and reach of government. The more they come to believe that, unless government does it, it won't be done.

Faulty reasoning. In the private sector, competition among suppliers induces people to solve problems, resulting in profits. The government sector, which has no profits, induces bureaucrats *not* to solve problems, since this would render their jobs unnecessary.

Say a constituent contacts his Congressional representative and demands, "If you don't enact a government benefit I want, I will vote you out of office."

Being limited to a single term, the representative can respond, "That's okay, I'll be leaving anyway."

The constituent can always arrange that the *successor* obtain what the constituent wants. But the chance of the constituent getting his way is far greater if his original representative remains in office for decades and learns the ways of government.

Members of Congress who remain in office for many years seem able to retire wealthy. They find ways to benefit financially from having political power. I don't mind people seeking office after they've gotten rich. I do mind them getting rich while in office. (You've come a long way down the governmental road from Scranton, haven't you, Mr. Biden?)

I would prefer that members of Congress be paid nothing except their expenses. But this would prevent the non-rich from running. I therefore suggest that the members be paid a salary equal to the lowest income included in the third quintile of the national income.

Divide the peoples' income into five equal parts, from low to high. The lowest two quintiles are clearly too low. The lowest income of the third quintile seems about right to me, a little below the median. People from the lowest income group would gain a step-up in pay. People from the middle and upper middle classes, would, for two or six years, have a lesser income. This doesn't mean they'd be unwilling to run. With the stakes of holding office considerably reduced, the cost of running for office would also fall. People would eventually run for office because they feel it's their turn to serve, especially after they've retired from their jobs.

If members of Congress can't bear the thought of their income being lower-middle, here's an alternative: Their pay raises could be limited to the lower of the CPI or 3%, but with no raise at all if the federal government ran a deficit in the previous fiscal year. Better yet, if the national debt in the previous year increased by 5%, the compensation to members of Congress would be reduced by 5%.

Members of Congress should certainly be subject to the same laws, regulations, and retirement programs that are imposed on everyone else. This is not the case today. The elite consider it beneath thcir station to be treated the same as riff raff like us.

A politician can consider himself a political professional only by continuing to be elected time after time. For this, campaign gifts are vital. The rich, including unions, tort lawyers, and corporations, are the ones with the cash. After donors supply the cash, the representative naturally wants to look out for the donors' political needs. The result is crony capitalism. The huge lobbying industry is right there to assist on how best to help them.

Government is supposed to help the poor, right? A substantial part of the money raised is siphoned off to political cronies and to the 2.8 million bureaucrats whose compensation, including benefits, is higher than that of the average American. Only a small portion reaches the poor.

The long-term results of government policies are usually counterintuitive. Money that does reach the poor, in the long run, makes them poorer. But money that reaches the crony capitalists is not counterintuitive: It works just fine and makes them richer. Why the difference I do not know.

While in office, the one-term members of Congress should get rid of the laws and regulations that cause long-term harm and add to the nation's debt. How many such requirements are there? When the sections, subsections, subsubsections, subsubsubsections, and subsubsubsubsections of the laws and regulations are taken into account, I'm guessing there are millions of distinctive uses of force among all levels of American government, most of them harmful.

Wiping these out just at the federal level would probably take several years. After the job is completed, Congress might comfortably remain in session for only a few weeks a year. The lobbying industry, one hopes, would be reduced to practically nothing.

Stop Funding Universities

Many of the ideas that have resulted in our enormous government were generated in universities. All governments of the United States should stop funding all universities.

Ideas flow from whence the money comes. Government makes no profits. The self-esteem of government leaders and bureaucrats depends on their taking action, trying to do good for society. Professors are unaware that many of these actions in the long run actually harm society. Nor do they *want* to know it, because they'd have to consider most of their ideas about public affairs worthless. Instead, they hope to become the advisors of those in power, helping to wield the power.

Tenure should be done away with. This is usually awarded by schools, not by government, supposedly to preserve freedom of thought. But this doesn't make tenure a good idea. Professors with tenure can soar into the blue with ideas that have no relation whatsoever to reality.

As Thomas Sowell put it, "Ideas that don't work are concentrated in institutions where ideas don't have to work to survive."

Universities foster a big grievance industry. Anyone speaking or writing ideas that discomfort liberals is unacceptable.

Universities also foster a big identity industry. If you're not a healthy, heterosexual, white, Anglo-Saxon, Protestant man, you're probably a victim of someone who is. Our kind and caring government, the professors believe, offers to look out for you. Fat chance!

Most of the professors care not a whit for the Constitution, which limits the power of government. They want government to wield more power, not less.

In the last thirty years, colleges built elaborate student centers and other facilities, hired armies of administrators, and raised tuitions enormously, making higher education less accessible to the poor. But the quality of college education has deteriorated. It's considered racist to teach Shakespeare, Western civilization, and American government. Better to teach black studies and women's studies, helping students to consider themselves victims. Except for the sciences, teaching students to become productive citizens has become secondary. Some faculty members may not even want students to become productive citizens because they'd be more likely to vote Republican.

We should abolish the Department of Education, encourage apprenticeship programs, and encourage for-profit schools. Let universities sink or swim on their own, raising money as needed from the private sector.

Abolish the Civil Service

Early U.S. presidents often hired assistants who had helped them attain power. The president had complete control over those who worked in the executive branch. It was called the "spoils system." The people thus hired did not expect the jobs to last for long. When a new president came in, especially from another political party, everyone was replaced by a new batch of people. The system was overtly corrupt. But the bureaucracy was small and did little harm.

Enter the Pendleton Civil Service Reform Act of 1883. This created a bureaucracy whose qualifications were based on merit, not on whom they had helped attain power.

Merit enables people to do their jobs better. But since the net long-term effects of most government jobs are negative, employee merit causes that much more damage.

The federal bureaucracy now numbers 2.8 million people, of whom only 2% are subject to the president's direct control. Their salaries and benefits are some 70% higher than those of people with equivalent jobs in the private sector. They're almost impossible to fire, usually retaining their jobs until death or retirement.

Having no profit by which to measure their self-esteem, bureaucrats do what they can, however subtly, to expand their budgets and expand their opportunities to exercise power. They try to influence laws to make those expansions possible.

The November 16, 2019 article from AIER, *Birth of the Deep State: A History,* written by economist Peter C. Earle, contains a description of the federal bureaucracy. I quoted this in *America's Governments, Enemies of the Poor* and quote it again here:

"The major functions of the bureaucracy are to thwart political measures it collectively deems unpalatable and to vigilantly protect the existence of the greater body within which it thrives.

"No orders are issued, and there is no chain of command. It communicates by example: leaks reported in the news beget more leaks; anonymous tips spawn a rash of new tipsters. No lofty conspiracy theories are necessary; a massive army of bureaucrats in an era of free/highly affordable burner phones, file-sharing services, and document-scanning apps are more than sufficient to gum up the wheels of executive action.

"There are no secret codes, no dead drops, and no shadowy agents meeting in parking garages in the dead of night. Perhaps more dauntingly, the deep state coalesces from among a seemingly incalculable number of nondescript men and women with families and homes in the Virginia and Maryland suburbs of Washington, DC. (The deep state) receives a salary every two weeks, drawn upon the United States Treasury. Its atomic elements—individuals—coach Little League, go to Zumba classes, and generally have mainstream opinions. Many, no doubt, dismiss the very notion of a deep state. Even when they send an anonymous email, shred a document intended for other eyes, or impishly pass a tip to someone with a second- or third-hand relationship in the media, most of them probably see the deep state as something larger, above and beyond themselves.

"Yet they are the deep state."

Dr. Ben Carson, formerly a successful brain surgeon, spent four years as secretary of Housing and Urban Development in the Trump administration. In a recent Glenn Beck televised interview, he said the swamp is much deeper and wider than he had expected. Federal bureaucrats care more about the positions they hold and the circumstances of the entire bureaucracy than they do about the American people they're supposed to be helping. Young people joining the bureaucracy with the intention of doing good for the people are demonized. When President Trump's policies greatly reduced unemployment among blacks and Hispanics, the bureaucrats considered this threatening. Needless to say, they hated that disrupter, Donald Trump.

America's founding fathers were all too familiar with government bodies whose powers were so concentrated that they made, interpreted, and administered laws all by themselves. The founders wisely split those functions into three separate branches of government: Congress, the courts, and the administration.

Some current bureaucrats provide all three functions themselves. It's too much concentration of power.

Although the corruption of the civil service is indirect, the system does far more long-term harm to society than the old-time spoils system. To drain the swamp, the Civil Service should be abolished.

Abolish the Federal Reserve Bank

Murray Rothbard's "A History of Money and Banking in the United States" reveals that, right from the beginning in 1776, excessive involvement in monetary affairs by the government caused inflationary booms that benefited crony capitalists and the elite, followed by busts. The people at the bottom of the heap were usually the first to be fired during downturns.

The attempt to manage the economy from the top down cannot

help but fail. Since its inception over a hundred years ago, the Federal Reserve Bank has done tremendous harm to America by unintentionally creating steep downturns in the economy. This has hurt everyone, but especially the poor. The Fed should be abolished, a matter considered in greater detail in Chapter 3.

Regulations

Regulations are far more costly than people realize. The cost of 2018 regulations is estimated to be $1.9 trillion—greater than both personal and corporate income tax revenues combined. The annual cost of compliance comes to about $2,500 per person. Regulations block innovation, devote resources to compliance instead of growth, and suppress employment.

Regulated companies, being subject to governmental force, are likely to figure out what they can get away with. If the same companies become subject mostly to free market capitalism, they would make an effort to avoid lawsuits. But they would be more likely to do what's right. Minimum standards of behavior would become reasonable standards of behavior.

The Federal Register is the official daily publication of the rules, proposed rules, and notices of federal agencies and organizations, as well as executive orders and other presidential documents. The annual number of pages in the Federal Register is a good indicator of the growth and impact of government. At the end of the Eisenhower administration in 1959, the pages numbered about 10,000. At the end of the Obama administration in 2015, they numbered about 97,000.

The administration during which the pages of the Federal Register increased by the greatest percentage was that of Richard Nixon. Nixon was a Republican, of course, but he was a certifiable RINO (Republican in Name only).

Congress should make the laws, not bureaucrats.

Reduce the Size of America's Government Sector to 10% of the GDP

To keep America's government from growing again, all levels of U.S. government must be cut back. In 2019, expenditures of the entire government sector constituted 35.7% of the GDP. More than one-third of the nation's economy consists of spending by the sector that produces no wealth and causes considerable harm. This is outrageous.

All schools should be privatized. Some would be operated for profit, others not, but none should be operated by government. With this change alone, local governments would be much reduced, with the nation much benefited.

Back in the 1890s, government occupied only 10% of the GDP. There was poverty in America in the 1890s, in some places even cholera. But most of the poverty was among new immigrants. Unlike the America of today, morale was high, and feelings of optimism were widespread. People quickly rose out of poverty and entered the middle class.

We should return the government sector to just 10% of the GDP, with a big reduction in the number of government departments.

Income should be taxed at a low, flat rate. This would require numerous Americans who currently pay no income tax to begin doing so. But there would be no FICA tax. (The FICA tax is regressive. A low flat tax on earnings is not.) There would be no tariffs, no capital gains taxes, no death taxes, no sales taxes, and no excise taxes. Just a low, flat income tax would be a huge improvement.

Stop Collecting Statistics

Government's collection of statistics uncovers economic and social problems that political leaders and bureaucrats hanker to solve. In the long run, they fail to solve them because the hidden hand of government eventually causes unintended harm to society. Let people in the private sector pay for the statistics they need.

Wars

Wars are usually the biggest contributors to national debts. The common people do not make wars. They have an influence, of course, but individually, people have neither the money nor the inclination to fight wars.

It is governments that make wars. They're the ones that borrow the money, own the weapons, and hire the warriors. Governments and perhaps the media can characterize foreign threats in such a way as to induce the people to do the fighting.

Doing away with the State Department and all of its embassies would help. Modern information technology has rendered them obsolete. America's representatives abroad should be tourists and, more importantly, those who engage in trade. No foreign representatives should be recognized by the U.S. government. Foreign policy should be conducted mainly by the president, the Defense Department, and interested citizens.

I'm not convinced that America needs its enormously expensive aircraft carrier fleets. We don't need to prove over and over that we can win World War II.

But the United States should certainly dominate space, to protect America from missiles from on high.

American business should spend as much effort as necessary to prevent foreign invasion of its computer programs.

We should tell Kim Jong-un and tell the world that if Kim or his military are responsible for the death of Americans, we will not conduct a war against North Korea. Instead, from land, from sea, or from space, our military will find and kill *him.*

China may be too powerful to be given such a threat. When it comes to foreign policy, I am probably out of my depth. I do find it disturbing that in the Defense Department's war games between the U.S. and China, the U.S. is consistently the loser.

As to defense, here's the big picture:

- China's dictatorship and top-down economic management will in the long run weaken China and eventually weaken its military.

- With a libertarian government, the American people will thrive. The nation's GDP will advance smartly, and this will enable its military to become ever more powerful. Even if the defense budget remains at 3% of the GDP, but the GDP itself doubles or triples, the U.S. military would be very powerful indeed. One hopes it will be used less and less in foreign operations. But being powerful in itself deters foreign encroachment.

As to the benign duties government should continue to fulfill, please turn to the next section.

WHAT A LIBERTARIAN GOVERNMENT SHOULD DO

Most laws and government regulations are counterintuitive. They're intended to do good, but in the long run they cause damage that far outweighs any initial good. The government duties and laws described in this section, however, are not counterintuitive. They're benign. They're intended to do good, and they succeed.

First, the proper duties of the federal government. There are only two:

1. Defend the Nation

This is a biggie, of course, currently comprising 3.2% of the GDP. During the Reagan administration, defense grew to 5% of the GDP. The Soviet Union, already half-dead, couldn't compete with the U.S. and folded altogether.

Fortunately, the United States has created a space force, whose primary function should be to establish overwhelming power and control in space. Enhancing the effectiveness of other U.S. forces on earth should be secondary.

The Defense Department has adopted too many woke liberal notions of late. It should forget about racism and economic equality; those matters are not its business. The military should bolster its meritocracy and stick to defense.

2. Establish and Enforce Immigration Laws

Many people immigrating to America come from countries whose governments are damaging to the civil rights and economies of their citizens. Being accustomed to big government, they tend to vote for Democrats. The Democrats favor open borders because they want the votes of as many immigrants as possible. Immigrants in immediate need of government services are especially desirable to the Democrats.

Renowned economist Milton Friedman said, "It's just obvious that you can't have open borders and a welfare state."

The only thing that's obvious to Democrats is their desire for a voting majority.

The goal should be to cut the size of government, not increase it. We should suppress the immigration of people in immediate need of government services. Immigrants skilled in science and technology, however, are highly desirable.

If too many immigrants are allowed in, all other things being equal, the income of citizens already here will be lower. If too few immigrants are allowed, the economy is weakened for the lack of dynamism and the dearth of workers.

To remove governmental discretion, which usually works out badly, I suggest that, each year, the then-current population of America be increased 1% or 2% by immigration.

State Laws Alone

It's up to the states to enact and enforce election laws. In 2020, some states fell down on the job in this regard. In six or seven states, the governorships and, in certain counties and cities, the local governments, courts, and police departments, had been controlled for years by the Democratic Party, enabling the presidential election of 2020 to be stolen.

The crooked voting machines should certainly be replaced.

State and Local Laws

State and local governments are where basic criminal laws are made. If you look carefully, you might find a law that goes like this:

"Thou shalt not murder, steal, or do bad things unless you're a Black Lives Matter guy breaking into a store to take stuff home. Then it's okay."

A law wouldn't say this, of course, but a combination of laws, regulations, and enforcements can add up to something similar, especially in Democratic states such as Washington and Oregon, where considerably more unrestrained rioting has occurred than has been reported in most news outlets.

Black Lives Matter opposes nuclear families, wants to abolish the police, and believes the Christian cross is a symbol of white supremacy. These views have been scrubbed from its website, but the organization continues to hold them. Genuine Americana, right?

State and local governments have the primary job of protecting private property and fostering individual liberty, duties that are essential. Freedom does not mean one can do whatever one wants. It means freedom from unlimited government.

Local governments and to a lesser extent the states should prevent people from directly hurting others by force or fraud. This is the police power. No matter who owns the property, the police should protect it, including that of corporations.

Some police duties should be delegated to the people. This excellent idea is discussed in Chapter 6.

The Courts

On a day-to-day basis, military training, the courts, and the police are the most active parts of a libertarian government. It is the courts that have the essential duties of enforcing contracts and adjudicating lawsuits. American courts have performed these duties reasonably well, a reason why the nation has thrived.

To reduce frivolous lawsuits, the losing side should be required to pay the legal costs of both sides.

Some say the enforcement of contracts and adjudication of lawsuits should be taken over by mediators in the private sector. This would be fine with me. The more the reduction of government, the better.

A Libertarian Society

More than a third of America's current Gross Domestic Product is government spending. Government is almost exclusively force. Force is a form of violence. With government so big, violence pervades the fabric of the nation.

"Pervade" is the perfect word. It means that "an influence, a feeling, or a quality is present and apparent throughout."

When government hands out money, you may say, "That's not violent."

Yes, it is. To a large extent, the money is obtained by taxation, which is backed by force. "Hand over your money, buster, or your goose is cooked."

The paying out of government money also constitutes force. This group over here can receive money. That group over there cannot. The selectivity arouses resentment and envy among the groups that don't receive the money, and there's nothing they can do about it except lobby, which is expensive.

A goodly portion of the money paid out by government is added to the national debt, with no plans for paying it off. The debt builds faster than other government expenses until the interest required to support the debt overwhelms the funds available, and the nation has to declare bankruptcy. Unless the extraordinary measures recommended in this chapter are adopted, bankruptcy will force us or our descendants into misery.

Americans expect each generation to have a better life than the last. This works only when the debt is low and government handouts are insignificant. Those thresholds have probably been passed.

When force pervades the nation, the natural response is to try to beat the system. Big government promotes selfishness. Everyone is out for himself or herself.

Libertarian government evokes altruism—the perfect word, meaning "the belief in or practice of disinterested and selfless concern for the well-being of others."

"You mean to tell me that in a free-market economy, everyone's going to have a selfless concern for the well-being of others?"

Not everyone, of course. But with government backed off, a growing number, especially among the prosperous, will develop such concerns. People will learn and change, becoming ever more concerned about others. With tax rates much reduced, people would also have the wherewithal to do something about their concerns.

Many television shows have portrayed wealthy businessmen as bad guys. Most are not. The preeminent bad guys are government and its nefarious partners, unions.

Many government programs are enacted on the basis that a certain group can't get along without the government's help, a point of view most often applied to blacks. Believing that blacks can't get along without government help implies that blacks are unable to help themselves. That's pure racism. Of *course* blacks can get along without government's help. An increasing number of blacks want government to just get the hell out of the way.

Government officials feel threatened by citizens insisting on taking responsibility for their own actions. Bureaucrats are inclined to believe that *they* are responsible for the welfare of citizens. They want problems to deal with. They are unaware, and fervently choose to remain unaware, that the use of force in the long run makes life more difficult and more expensive for most people, but especially for the poor.

The long term is the primary term that government should be concerned with. After a law or a regulation is enacted, problems eventually result. The government then enacts what it believes is a solution to those problems. But the solution also causes problems, which comingle with those caused previously. It's a downward cycle. No one knows what's causing what. Bureaucrats make sure to keep their blinders on to avoid seeing anything that might necessitate cutting their budgets.

Walter Williams: "Most of the great problems we face are caused by politicians creating solutions to problems they created in the first place."

That's it exactly.

Many people feel that if government steps away from (supposedly) helping the poor, the help would not be provided by anyone.

Nonsense. We already have a governmental superstructure that's intended to help the poor. Part of it consists of politicians buying votes, but not all of it by any means. Rich people in America genuinely believe it's not right for them to thrive while some Americans are in poverty. This makes them feel guilty, which in this case is a good thing.

The rich are willing to part with some of their money so the government can take care of those in need. The rich want a safety net for the non-rich.

But the government does a wretched job of it. Some of the money goes back to the crony capitalists, because those are the people whose campaign gifts keep the professional politicians in power. Some of the money sticks with the government itself. It's not that the bureaucrats steal the money. But there are millions of them, and they have to eat. They're paid handsomely, making the zip codes around Washington, DC the wealthiest zip codes in the nation. A minority of the money reaches the poor, along with uses of force that make their lives more difficult and more expensive.

The point is, the rich want a safety net, and they're willing to part with some of their money to obtain it. The charitable impulse is there. That's the main thing.

Here's the sticking point: The rich want someone *else* to help the poor, namely the government. But this is a lesser problem. It's not too much of a step for them to realize that the safety net can and should be supplied by people from within the private sector.

Some prosperous people might feel, "I believe we should have a safety net, and I might be persuaded to do something about it. But I'm not so sure my neighbor would be willing to do the same."

No doubt that's true in some cases. But have faith. The desire for a safety net is indeed widespread. If the people of the United States would realize that government is the worst way to obtain a safety net—that government's use of force creates more problems than it solves—the way would be open for the safety net to be achieved from the private sector. The prosperous would only need to encourage and help finance those who want to do the work. Many will want to make a living doing it. Those who help others have to eat too.

But the living costs of private citizens who want to provide the safety net are tiny in comparison with the stupendous cost of government, especially since those providing the help would be in competition with one another.

The safety net providers would get to know the individuals who need help. They might encourage a single young woman, for example, to obtain an education, get a job, and avoid having a child until she's married. No end of social good can come of such help.

Getting wealthy people to understand all this is not impossible. The hard job is already done: They want a safety net for the indigent. They can readily learn that the job can remain in the private sector and be performed better and less expensively than by government. There would still be reasonable inequality of wealth, because some people are natural money-makers and others are not. But there would be few indigents.

With the huge government superstructure disassembled, the top tax rates could be cut way back. Everyone would be subject to a low, flat income tax rate and no other tax. Plenty of money would be available for the private sector to provide a safety net, with money left over. Don't tell anyone, but eventually, a libertarian society might do away with coercive taxation altogether. All government revenues would be voluntary gifts.

Sharply limiting government would raise morale, increase self-reliance and care, and improve the quality of life across the land. The poor would flourish. Competition among those who are providing care would minimize costs.

The more needs that arise, the more people would come forward to meet them. Even a nation as large as ours could become a giving society, propelled by the feeling that we're all in this together.

CHAPTER 2
The Economy

THE BEST MONETARY SYSTEM

THERE ARE TWO MAJOR AREAS of American life in which competition does not operate. Both are disasters.

One is healthcare. Except for modest co-pays, people don't pay each time they obtain healthcare services. It is government or the insurance companies that pay, right from the first dollar of the user's cost. The healthcare users therefore don't care what the costs are, and there's little need for the suppliers to compete with one another. As a result, the nation's healthcare costs are about twice what they should be. This issue is discussed in more detail in Chapter 5.

The other area of American life in which competition does not operate is the U.S. dollar. The government imposes a monopoly on its currency. Debts must be paid in dollars (well, maybe a little with bitcoins).

It has not worked out well. Under the Federal Reserve's monetary management, the value of the dollar has fluctuated greatly. When the dollar's value falls, sellers are hurt and buyers are helped. When the dollar's value rises, buyers are hurt and sellers are helped. A steady diet of these fluctuations has created difficulties for the people and made the economy more volatile.

When the dollar's value falls, debtors are helped and creditors are hurt. The biggest debtor in the world is the U.S. government. Needless to say, it is partial to the dollar's deterioration, a big reason why the management of the nation's monetary system should be delegated to the people.

In addition to short-term fluctuations, the value of the dollar over the long term has deteriorated sharply. The Fed has no limit on its creation of dollars, which is why the dollar's value has deteriorated so much over the years.

(The banks have some limit on how many dollars they can create, because they're required to hold a portion of their deposits on reserve at the Federal Reserve Bank.)

The government should remove the dollar monopoly. Anything, including the dollar, could serve as legal tender. Whoever creates a currency would have to mint cash and coin, which is no easy matter. The best existing paper currency is the Swiss franc. People could trade warehouse receipts for gold, just as they do for commodities. Morgan Dollars and BankAmerica Dollars would work just fine.

Americans could have a bank account in any currency, as long as a bank is willing to create it. Each currency must be exchangeable in free markets with all of the others.

You might find it burdensome to have several bank accounts in different currencies. But before the Euro came into being, the Europeans lived with this for years.

In the 1980s, I had occasion to have lunch with Colman M. Mockler, Jr., who was CEO of the Gillette Company from 1975 until his death in 1991. I asked him how difficult it would be for Americans to own bank accounts in various currencies. His answer: "I don't think that would be a serious problem."

All banks benefit from the creation of money. It costs the bank virtually nothing to credit your account with a loan. When you later repay the loan, the money disappears. The interest you pay is the bank's profit. That money does not disappear. It came from you; the bank did not create it. The profit is called "seigniorage." Banks love seigniorage. Central banks like it too, which is one reason why they're reluctant to give up being central banks.

Here's the key: Without the Federal Reserve, currencies would be in competition with one another as to whether they retain their buying power and their convenience. If banks create too many Morgan Dollars, for example, the buying power of that currency would deteriorate, and people would stop using it. The banks would want to avoid this, because they would no longer earn seigniorage.

The system is self-regulatory. No overriding government is needed to protect the value of a currency (which they're not doing all that well anyway). Competition does the job without anyone serving as regulator.

Banks who create currencies would not need to set policies. No bank, for example, needs to declare that the economy currently needs such-and-such currency to be increased by a certain percentage. If the statement is correct, the bank's customers would request loans in that currency, and this would do the job without a policy statement from anyone. The economy would be guided by people simply meeting their own needs and adjusting to supply and demand.

The principal function of the creators of a currency is to keep the general price level the same. The competition between currencies accomplishes this. With the Federal Reserve Bank gone, monetary policy is delegated to the people. But the people wouldn't make policy or plan anything other than for themselves. They're just living. Competition between the currencies would become the automatic regulator.

Level values of the currencies are of paramount importance. Having several currencies in competition with one another keeps them level. After a time, it's likely that one currency would prevail. But when the management of that currency changes and it begins to lose value, the people would switch to another.

BITCOINS: FINE AS SPECULATIONS

Bitcoins are fine as speculations. But people who use them as a means of exchange in a significant way will probably go broke. Here's why:

Person A owns an Item he doesn't need. He'd rather have dollars.

Person B has dollars she doesn't need. She'd rather have the Item.

If the Federal Reserve Bank no longer exists, A and B would have to agree on which currency to use—probably an easy decision. With all this determined, the trade is a go.

The main variables are the exact nature of the Item and the price. During the seconds, minutes, hours, or days when the transaction is planned, neither A nor B wants to bother with changes in the value of the currency.

During the trading day, the value of bitcoins changes significantly about every few seconds. If bitcoins replaced dollars as the means of exchange, the transaction would probably not occur at all,

Another problem with bitcoins: inconvenience. In a cursory review of the Internet, I could not determine the total number of dollar transactions that occur in America every day. But the following are snippets I did learn:

The New York Stock Exchange trades two to six billion shares of stock every day. (The number of *transactions* is fewer than the number of shares, of course. But it's still a lot, and this doesn't include other exchanges.)

300,000 futures transactions take place every day.

108 million credit card transactions take place every day, the majority probably in dollars.

In 2015, the Federal Reserve processed 14 trillion financial transactions every day. What those consisted of I do not know, but it was certainly a great many.

Match all those transactions against this: The mining and

verification of a single bitcoin transaction takes an average of 10 minutes and sometimes up to a week.

Not all that convenient, I would say.

The *amount* of money available must change modestly on a second-to-second basis to keep the *values* of the currencies level. This would occur naturally because of transactions by millions the people with bank-managed currencies that are in competition with one another.

Bitcoins are much too inflexible. They're fine as speculations, but using them as the primary currency would render the economy deader than a doornail.

Elon Musk plans to accept bitcoins as payments for Tesla cars. Maybe he knows something I don't know. He probably does. His mother said that when Elon was nine years old, he read the entire Encyclopedia Britannica and *remembered* it!

RESULTS OF HIGHER TAX RATES

November 15, 2020. Mr. Moderate, Don't-Call-Me-a-Socialist Joe Biden wants to raise income tax rates, capital gains rates, and death tax rates.

Little does he know that in the long run, the government's tax *revenues* would not rise; they would fall.

No one in government, even mighty Joe, controls its tax revenues. That's for the citizens to determine. They alone control their reactions to changes in tax rates.

Income Taxes

With the approval of Congress, Biden intends to raise the top tax rate on personal income from 37% to 51%, forcing the rich to pay the share of their income that Biden considers fair.

To illustrate the impact of this, let's say you're in the top bracket, and you earn $100. The tax would be $51, leaving you with $49. $51 is 104% of the $49 you'd have left. Pretty heavy burden.

In the short run—say, within a few months—the government's revenues would rise, especially if the increase in tax rates applies retroactively.

Liberals picture rich people having big piles of cash, which they greedily and regularly count. That picture may apply to unions, which are loaded with cash ready to be handed out as campaign gifts. But people in the higher tax brackets would react in ways Mr. Biden may not expect.

Rather than hold cash, most rich people invest their money in businesses. If they're taxed too heavily, they would reduce those interests to cut their taxable income. Some would limit how much they work. Some CEOs would call off selling a bond (a corporate IOU) that would have enabled the company to expand. Some would decide to close up shop and retire prematurely, telling employees, maybe all of their employees, "I'm sorry, but I'm going to have to let you go." All this makes the entire society poorer.

Such reactions take a while to settle in. But eventually they do, and the economy slows. Even if the high tax rates remain in place, the amount of income to which the high rates apply falls and the government's revenues therefore drop to a level below that which prevailed before the tax rates were raised.

With the economy weak, the rate of unemployment would rise. Those at the lowest income levels would suffer the most because they're usually the first to be laid off.

Recall that when President Trump lowered tax rates, the income of blacks and Hispanics rose faster than the income of those at higher levels. If Biden raises tax rates, the income of blacks and Hispanics would *fall* faster than the income of those at higher levels. This would be government's diabolic hidden hand in operation, as follows:

In the long run, the actual results of most uses of government force are opposite to the intended results. Big government spending causes the wealth of the poor to grow more slowly or decrease faster than that of the rich.

Congress starts hearing from the folks at home. "The people are hurting. We have to start sending them government money the Fed creates out of nothing." The freebie government handouts would raise the amount of money in circulation. But the economy is producing fewer goods and services to buy. Things that once cost $10 now cost $12. "Inflation," they call it. The buying power of savings diminishes, and the retirement incomes of Americans are worsened.

Mighty Joe thought he was raising taxes. He didn't. He just raised the *rates*. This draws a bigger portion of the economy into the maws of government, which produces no wealth. The economy is thus weakened, causing the government's revenues eventually to go down, not up.

The phrase "increase taxes" creates nothing but confusion. It's the *rates* that are raised. This weakens the economy and eventually reduces the revenues.

The opposite is also true: Lowering the tax rates leaves more money in the productive private sector and less in the unproductive government sector. The economy is strengthened, thus raising the tax revenues.

Besides, the freebie handouts that Biden has in mind make the recipients feel dependent and worthless. Far better that they be employed in a vibrant economy.

Capital Gains

Biden wants the top long-term capital gains tax rate to soar from 24% to 40%. He wants those rich guys to give back some of what he considers their ill-gotten gains. (I understand your family has accumulated some $30 million of ill-gotten gains, Joe. In your case, I guess it's okay, right?)

If the top capital gains do rise substantially, you don't suppose that investors who hold profitable stocks will sell them right off and enable the government to claim a huge portion, do you? Of course they won't. They'll hold on to those suckers for dear life, hoping that some day the rates will fall. If they die in the meantime, each security would have a new tax basis—the value as of the date of death. This means the capital gain incurred prior to death is wiped out and never taxed. True, the date-of-death value is subject to the death tax. But the capital gains embedded within the death value is not subject to the capital gains tax as well.

Death Taxes

Mr. Biden also wants to raise the top death tax rate. People with significant funds won't take this lying down (except at the funeral and thereafter). Death taxes are enormously complicated. Tax lawyers will sharpen their pencils to even finer points and figure out ways to legally avoid the higher taxes. Death taxes produce no government revenues in excess of the cost of enforcing them.

But farmers will get hit hard. A big portion of their estates consists of the value of their land. Instead of passing the farm to children desirous of working the land, their estates might have to sell the land, or at least a big chunk of it, to raise sufficient cash for the hefty death tax. The government won't accept land in payments. It wants cash.

Government takes cash from some and redistributes it to others, keeping a pretty hefty portion for itself along the way. This is why the zip codes around Washington, DC are the nation's wealthiest.

HOW TO ACHIEVE ZERO TAX REVENUES

There are two ways that government can have zero income-tax revenues:*

1. The tax rate is zero. The government takes not a penny from anyone. The economy flourishes but, except for voluntary gifts, government revenues are for naught. For some reason, governments don't cotton to this approach.

2. The tax rate is 100%, the government takes every penny of income that people report. But the people report no income. Everyone becomes a criminal, operating underground. The economy comes close to dying, and government revenues are zero. (During World War II, Franklin Roosevelt wanted to set the top tax rate on income at 100%. Congress didn't go along and made it 90% instead. People generally accept higher tax rates during the threat of war than they do in peacetime.)

Successful governments try to guess the rate of tax the people prefer to pay, enabling the government's revenues to be maximized. (People abide high tax rates in wartime. In peacetime, not so much.)

Liberals usually set the rates higher than the level the people are most willing to pay. With the rates too high, citizens take evasive measures to avoid paying the excessive tax. The liberals then turn the screws to increase compliance, which raises the nation's level of stress.

Generally, the liberals want the rates high, so that an ever larger portion of the nation's income will flow through their hands, increasing their domination over society.

---

*Thanks to economist Arthur Laffer.

HIDDEN HANDS OF GOVERNMENT

A major achievement of the Trump administration was to increase the supply side of the economy. Yes, he cut personal income tax rates a little. But his main effort was to cut corporate tax rates substantially and reverse numerous Obama regulations that had throttled production. This encouraged the economy's supply side. He also enabled corporations to transfer to America the profits they'd earned abroad without incurring excessive tax, further improving supply.

With the supply side unleashed, businesses thrived. Corporations hired millions of people, which in turn increased demand.

Liberals don't much care about the supply side. They assume that helping corporations enables money-grubbing capitalists to keep their profits, widening the gap between rich and poor.

Wrong. The owners of corporations can't enjoy higher profits themselves without hiring workers, thus spreading the money around. The owners do benefit, of course, but mostly because of the higher price of the stocks they own. A great many Americans own stocks in their pension plans. Strengthening the supply side helps them too.

Liberals' favorite way to increase demand is to hand out cash. This supposedly enables people to buy the goods they need. But if the production of goods is suppressed, as above, goods aren't available for purchase. The extra cash thus causes inflation.

The results proved the correctness of Trump's policies. Millions of people were hired. The number of those working reached record high levels. The income of people with low wages increased faster than those with higher wages, and inflation stayed low.

Why did the poor benefit more than the rich?

I don't know why. I can only repeat the intuition I've often written: Increasing freedom from government enables the poor to gain wealth faster than the rich.

Economist Milton Friedman said, "The society that puts equality before freedom will end up with neither. The society that puts freedom before equality will end up with a great measure of both."

In 1776, the year America declared its independence, Adam Smith, a Scottish economist, published his foundational book, "The Wealth of Nations." He was the first to refer to the "hidden hand" of free markets, which provide indirect and unintended benefits to society.

I too have written about the hidden hand of free markets. But I have also written what I have not read elsewhere: The hidden hand of *government* brings indirect and unintended *harm* to society.

TARIFFS AND PROTECTIONISM: BAD NEWS

The U.S. Constitution authorizes the president to apply tariffs. The president should decline the offer. Tariffs are a tax on the importation of goods, and they're always damaging.

Any effort by government to protect an industry does more harm than good. Let's say foreign companies that make steel are slapped with a tariff when exporting their products to the U.S. (President Trump did apply such a tariff early in his administration.) This raises the domestic price of steel, which benefits U.S. steelworkers. But the number of workers of companies that *use* steel outnumbers the steelworkers by about three times. With the prices of their products rising, some are laid off. The losses they suffer exceed the benefits enjoyed by the steelworkers.

If an exchange of goods and money does not benefit both parties of the trade, the trade is not made. All trades benefit both sides. It's okay even when a nation's imports exceed exports.

America has run trade deficits for most of its history. This didn't drain the nation of its wealth. Instead, we became one of the world's fastest-growing nations.

Since World War II, Hong Kong has set no tariffs on goods made in other countries, even when the other countries applied tariffs on goods made in Hong Kong. Regardless, Hong Kong reigned for many years as the world's fastest-growing economy.

America has a huge surplus in services. We sell considerably more property insurance, banking, and other services than we buy.

The deficit in *trade* captures attention. The surplus in services does not. The people who manufacture things that are part of the trade deficits are unionized, and they squawk a lot. The people who provide services are not unionized, and they squawk little.

The solution: get rid of the federal laws that support unions, as explained in a later chapter.

Tariffs and protectionism are always harmful. President Trump's tariffs were a mistake. He was much too cavalier about America's trade relationships.

The nation would be better off if all tariffs were cut to zero, even if the tariffs of other nations are not. We would gain wealth, not lose it. Economics are funny that way. They're counterintuitive.

STAKEHOLDER CAPITALISM

Liberals have come up with another great idea: stakeholder capitalism. This means corporations should not just attend to profits for their shareholders. They should also advance the interests of their customers, employees, suppliers, and communities.

But most corporations already advance the interests of their stakeholders. If they care not about their customers, they eventually won't have any. If they care not about their employees, production will fall. If they care not about their suppliers, the right materials won't show up on time to work with. If they care not about their communities, the communities won't care about them.

But this doesn't satisfy the liberal elites. Corporations must do more for the precious stakeholders.

Identifying *profits* isn't all that hard for corporations. Profits have dollar clarity and are evident in financial statements. But how can corporate managers determine exactly how much extra the company should spend on customers, employees, suppliers, and communities?

They don't know.

The liberal political elites don't know either. Nobody knows.

The best and fairest allocation is accomplished by free market pricing over a long period of time. That's the positive hidden hand of free market capitalism. It's the best way for companies and stakeholders to succeed. It's the only way the poor can gain wealth faster than the rich.

But the liberal elite hate to leave power in the hands of others, as they're forced to do when the allocation of resources is left to free markets. No, they want the power themselves.

Untroubled by not knowing exactly how much corporations should allocate to stakeholders, the liberal elite foster a concern for stakeholders to create confusion. They want corporations to seek the government's advice. Ah, this gives government the power.

(Franklin Roosevelt's method of governing was similar. He would ask one person to do a job and another person to do a similar job. Conflicts were inevitable, causing matters to bubble up to the president for resolution—just what FDR wanted.)

If Congress supports stakeholder capitalism, the corporations will comply to keep the government from putting them out of business. Compliant corporations will spend more of their resources on the stakeholders than they would have spent without the government's interference, eventually reducing their profits. In the long run, this will weaken the stakeholders. After a company fritters away its profits, it will have fewer resources to spend on the stakeholders than if the company had focused all along on its profits.

The managers of some of the largest corporations have not just complied; they've aligned themselves with government, perhaps in hopes of joining the liberal elite themselves. They're gung-ho on stakeholder capitalism. In addition, they've become arbiters of political speech. They've withheld essential services to people they consider conservative and partly shut down social media. Thanks, fellows, for making America not so great again.

Stakeholder capitalism is another harmful liberal idea that will make everyone equally poor.

Except for the liberal elites, of course. They'll be the most equal of all.

CUT PENSION PAYMENTS

Some Democratic states, like Illinois and California, are burdened with sky-high pension payments.

Solution: Reduce the pension payments.

"You can't do that," say the unions. "Those pensions were set by free market negotiations."

No, they weren't. Very little about unions is free market. Unions couldn't exist in their present form without the support of federal laws. In effect, the pensions were imposed by force.

Unjustifiably high, the pensions should be reduced. As discussed in Chapter 7, the laws that support unions should also be repealed.

THE COVID RELIEF BILL

December 28, 2020. The coronavirus relief bill that cleared Congress on December 21, 2020 was a $900 billion blockbuster. Before the votes were taken, the members of Congress were given only two hours to read its 5,593 pages. They can read fast, of course.

The title of the bill is misleading. The Covid virus is not the problem. The lockdowns and other measures adopted to deal with Covid were, and still are, the problem. They are devastating mistakes. The death rate of Covid-19 is lower than that of the SARS and H1N1 influenza in 2009, for which no lockdowns were imposed. Killing the economy has been unnecessary and extremely harmful.

This bill and its predecessor attempt to relieve the pain caused by the state lockdowns. But Congress felt entitled to throw in the kitchen sink as well, adding significantly to the nation's debt.

The main impetus for this bill was the extra $300 a week for eleven weeks to those receiving state unemployment benefits. States that locked down the hardest—NJ, CA, IL & NY—having higher unemployment, are rewarded for their misguided policies with larger federal payments.

The $300-a-week unemployment benefits will cost about $200 billion. For the other $700 billion, I learned about most of the provisions from regular news outlets, as follows:

The bill provides additional weeks of unemployment insurance for self-employed and gig economy workers—meaning those who work temporary jobs as independent contractors, typically in the service sector.

There's an extra benefit of $100 a week for people who are both self-employed and have salaried jobs.

Another round of direct payment checks was later issued for $600 for those making up to $75,000 a year and $1,200 for couples making up to $150,000 a year, plus $600 for each dependent child. This is half the amount provided by the Cares Act last March. But unlike that bill, these payments also go to illegal immigrants married to legal immigrants.

The family members of illegal aliens not only receive the $600 stimulus checks. They also receive the previous $1,200 given out in the March bill, making $1,800 in all.

There follows specific amounts for domestic needs:

$284 billion for first- and second-loans through the Paycheck Protection Program.

$13 billion for farmers and ranchers affected by the pandemic.

$25 billion in rental assistance to help pay for past due and future rent payments and utility bills.

Expansion of the program to include nonprofits and local news organizations, and an additional $20 billion of grants for businesses in low-income communities.

$15 billion loans for live entertainment venues, cultural institutions, and independent movie theaters, including churches.

$28 billion for the purchase and distribution of additional vaccines.

$22 billion to the states for Covid testing, tracing, and mitigation programs.

Over $3 billion for the Strategic National Stockpile of protective equipment and other supplies needed for responding to the pandemic.

$4 billion for substance abuse programs, mental health services, healthcare providers, and Covid-19 research.

$82 billion for schools, of which about $54 billion will go to K-12 schools. Many of the schools are closed, but the teachers' unions can always use the cash for congressional campaign contributions.

$1.7 billion for historically black colleges and universities, tribal colleges, and other minorities.

$10 billion for child care services.

$15 billion for airlines to pay some of the 32,000 U.S. airline workers who were furloughed after a six-month $25 billion bailout from the March bill that ran out at the end of September.

$14 billion for mass transit programs.

$10 billion "more" for state highways.

$1 billion for money-losing Amtrak.

$7 billion for broadband funding.

$300 million for rural broadband.

$250 million for telehealth.

$2 billion to replace foreign manufactured broadband equipment that poses national security threats.

$14 million for the Kennedy Center (on top of the $26 million it received from the previous relief bill). The building is closed, but I suppose Congress wants the curtain ready to rise immediately after reopening. Washington's elite, after all, must be suitably entertained.

Because of lobbying by Jerry Seinfeld, money is supplied for comedy clubs. No help, however, for restaurants and bars.

$1 billion for two new Smithsonian museums: the American Women's History Museum and the National Museum of the American Latino.

A 64-page section devoted to Horseracing Integrity and Safety.

Funds for studying the 1908 Springfield, Illinois race riot.

The specific amounts for domestic purposes above total $572 billion. Here, now, are lesser amounts for the rest of the world:

$4 billion for vaccination programs abroad.

$700 million to Sudan.

$500 million for Jordan's defense.

$74.8 million for a Caribbean Basic Security Initiative.

$33 million to support democracy in Venezuela.

$169 million for Vietnam.

$1.3 billion for Egypt.

$15 million to repair a military cutter in Sri Lanka.

$453 million for the Ukraine, source of several million for the forlorn Biden family.

$505 million to Belize, Costa Rica, El Salvador, Guatemala, Honduras, Nicaragua, and Panama to address key factors that contribute to the migration of unaccompanied, undocumented minors to the U.S.

$461 million to Colombia "for programs related to counter narcotics and human rights."

$150 million to Jordan for enhanced border security.

$100 million to Lebanon, Egypt, Tunisia, and Oman for enhanced border security.

$15 million for democracy programs and $10 million for gender programs in Pakistan.

Millions for Georgia, part of the old Soviet Union.

Money for India and other nations, invasive species mitigation, and water management on the Tibetan plateau.

The specific amounts above for interests abroad total $10 billion, making the sum of both domestic and foreign interests $582 billion. (This is short of $700 billion. I am unfamiliar with all of the bill's provisions.)

The Covid Relief Act, together with the Cares Act of March 2020, not only provides Covid relief, but also endeavors to reorder society. Money is taken from working taxpayers, or heavily borrowed, and given to those who aren't working. Social programs are expanded, the size and power of government is increased, and crony capitalists are well attended to. All of this is socialism.

Note how specific the measures are. This would be impossible, of course, except that the members of Congress know everything there is to know about everything.

The Senate vote was 92-to-6. The six who opposed were all Republicans. The Republicans who voted *for* the gargantuan bill have assured their constituents that, oh yes, they scrutinize every dollar of federal expenditures.

If Congress backed off, but limited House and Senate members to one term each, abolished the Civil Service, abolished the Federal Reserve Bank, sold the government's gold, land, roads, and the postal services, stopped collecting statistics, stopped funding universities and schools, sold the land it owns but doesn't itself utilize, applied a low, flat income tax, and greatly reduced the size of the federal government to 10% of the GDP, most of these needs would be met, and met far better, by private citizens who care.

CHAPTER 3
The Federal Reserve Bank: No Help at All

NO CENTRAL BANK NEEDED

THE GREEN CASH AND COINS we carry around are minted by the U.S. Treasury. But those are only about 3% of our money supply. Most of the money consists of numbers in bank accounts.

An important creator of the U.S. dollar has been the Federal Reserve Bank, the nation's central bank. The Fed doesn't even have to make a loan to create money. It has created so many dollars that their value has diminished substantially. An item bought for one dollar in 1913, when the Federal Reserve was created, would cost about $26 today.

America needs its medium of exchange to have a level value. Having failed in this, the Federal Reserve Bank should be abolished.

But we need the Fed to guide the economy, right?

No, we don't. The Fed has done a wretched job of guiding the economy. It tries to level out the excessive good times and the excessive bad times. But the poor old Fed doesn't know when the economy's in excess and when it isn't.

Nobody knows.

In its ignorance, the Fed has *caused* too many downturns, which are devastating for the poor. No economy can be guided successfully from the top down. Unguided, from the bottom up, the economy works fine, with minor disruptions in the short term and remarkable success in the long term.

The people of the world probably engage in many billions of financial transactions a day, with billions just in the United States. To do the job right, the central bank would have to know every one of them, which of course is impossible.

A free market economy doesn't just *know* about every financial transaction. The transactions, unimpeded by government, *are* the free market economy. The economy has no plan. It simply adjusts to what people need, what they buy and sell, borrow and lend. It adjusts to what people take from the sun, from the earth, and from plants. It adjusts to the harm they suffer from the wind, rain, snow, heat, cold, wars, pestilence, earthquakes, and volcanos. It adjusts to wants and excesses.

People do the best they can to meet their own needs. When necessary, people offer higher prices. Those who don't have the money can borrow or obtain help from elsewhere. With every transaction, both the buyers and the sellers endeavor to benefit themselves. The free market economy incorporates all these needs, trades, prices, and benefits without guidance. No matter how well intentioned, interference by authorities cannot help but make things worse.

If the Federal Reserve is abolished, as it should be, the Department of the Treasury and other federal departments could still interfere with the economy. We can't abolish the government altogether, of course, but voters should insist that government interfere as little as possible. When it interferes once, problems subsequently arise. No one knows whether the problems were caused by the interference or not. Just in case, they try to solve the problem. From the solutions, more problems result. Government should assume that any interference in the economy will cause more problems than it solves, because that's the truth.

The only proper task of a central bank is to maintain a level value of the dollar and keep the general price level constant. This the Federal Reserve Bank has not done—not even close.

After the Fed is abolished, the job of retaining a constant price level should be delegated to the people, as described in Chapter 2.

The Federal Reserve also regulates banks. One purpose is to prevent banks from taking excessive risk. Such regulation is unnecessary. The bank is likely to take as much risk as the regulator will allow it to get away with. If the bank starts to go under, the Fed is likely to help out to prevent the Fed from getting blamed for inadequate regulation.

Without regulation, the bank is more likely to adopt an appropriate level of risk, so the bank itself doesn't get the blame and lose customers.

Another purpose of the regulation: to make sure the bank isn't cheating its depositors. Again, this is unnecessary. The customers of unregulated banks will learn to pay attention to the possibility of their being cheated and complain loudly and publicly when they are. Banks that are stupid enough to cheat their customers will induce customers to stay away in droves.

But despite all this, banks will sometimes fail. If government has kept its hands off the economy, however, the level of debt will be relatively low. The economy will not be on tenterhooks, as it is now, and the failure will be isolated and not ruinous. Yes, some depositors may lose their money, but they will learn to become aware of what banks are doing with depositor money. Other banks may step in to help out to protect the industry.

Regulation also tends to freeze the industry's technology. Without regulation, banks are more likely to adopt changes that benefit the customers. (The freezing of technology has applied significantly to healthcare, with which the government has been heavily involved.)

Unregulated, free-market capitalism minimizes wrongdoing, risk, and rigidity.

THE FEDERAL RESERVE'S MISUNDERSTANDINGS

The managers and bureaucrats of the Federal Reserve Bank consistently hold to certain economic misunderstandings and errors. This section points out the errors, of course. But first it explains *why* the Federal Reserve continues to make them. What is it about working for government that so often makes people wrong?

The Federal Reserve Bank isn't exactly like other government agencies, but it's close. It was created in 1913 to serve as the nation's central bank. The most important function of a central bank is to provide the nation with the proper amount of its currency so that the general price level remains constant. The Federal Reserve's Board of Governors is an agency of the federal government and is directly accountable to Congress. Members of the board, appointed by the president and confirmed by the Senate, provide general guidance for the Federal Reserve System. Though Congress sets the goals for monetary policy, decisions of the Board and its subsidiary committees about how to reach those goals do not require approval by anyone in the executive or legislative branches. The Fed is not funded by congressional appropriations. Because of the seigniorage, no such appropriations are necessary (See Chapter 2).

Since the staff of the Fed is modeled on that of the U.S. Civil Service System, the characteristics and goals of its employees are similar to those of other government agencies, as follows:

- It is nearly impossible for bureaucrats to be fired.

- Including benefits, bureaucrats are paid considerably more than people with equivalent jobs in the private sector. This and the difficulty of being fired generate a we-they feeling. Bureaucrats lack empathy for the difficulties people in the private sector experience from the government's use of force. The Fed's manipulations of money constitute using force because citizens cannot avoid the Fed by using an alternative currency. Except possibly for bitcoins, the dollar is a monopoly.

- Unlike the private sector, bureaucrats do not generate profits by which to measure their self-esteem. The Fed's profits, which were $88.5 billion in 2020, are turned over to the Treasury Department and don't have the same emotional impact as profits generated in the private sector, in which profits can be retained or reinvested. The Federal Reserve's profit at $88.5 billion was half again higher than the highest net profit of any U.S. corporation, namely Apple, whose latest annual profit was $58.4 billion. This demonstrates the enormity of the amounts manipulated by the Fed.

- How do government workers measure their self-esteem? For one thing, they exercise power over others. Government is the only part of society that's authorized to use force. The Fed exercises force mostly by manipulating the number of dollars, by setting or influencing interest rates, and by its regulation of banks.

- Government employees increase their self-esteem by expanding their budgets and increasing the number of people who work for them. Having no profits, government workers care little about reducing expenses. Elections have almost no impact on costs. Government is the most expensive way to do anything. In contrast, private enterprises, striving to maximize profits, are inclined to minimize costs.

- Government workers also strive to avoid being blamed.

- They use wildly inaccurate computer models to scare the public, inducing people to abide by the recommendations of supposed experts. (Most Americans have been scared out of their wits about Covid-19, inducing them to accept the disastrous lockdowns.)

- Bureaucrats avoid actually solving social and economy problems, because this would render their jobs unnecessary.

"We're not concerned about those things," says the Fed. "We're just trying our best to make things better for the American people."

I'm sure you believe that, and I appreciate your good intentions. But to fulfill the above objectives, you consistently make errors that make the economy worse and more volatile. If you came down on the correct side of the issues, you'd be taking less action. In fact, you'd be taking no action except to keep the value of the dollar level.

When the Federal Reserve Bank takes responsibility for the well-being of the economy, people consider it the Fed's fault when the economy has a problem. (A corollary: When the government takes responsibility for the nation's health by adopting single-payer health insurance, it becomes the government's fault when anyone gets sick or dies.)

When something in the economy goes wrong, it's the Fed's fault. Yet the Fed hates being blamed. As a result, the Fed is constantly on tenterhooks. I would relieve them of this quandary by abolishing the Federal Reserve Bank altogether and letting go its 22,000 staff members, including the 400 PhD economists. But they don't seem to go for that solution.

Okay, here are errors I know of that the Federal Reserve Bank has made:

The Phillips Curve

Economist William Phillips described an apparent inverse relationship between unemployment and inflation. His explanation probably included an important curve in a graph, causing his theory to be dubbed the "Phillips Curve."

Here's how the theory goes: On some occasions, economic weakness raises unemployment and reduces inflation. On other occasions, economic strength lowers unemployment and increases inflation. Unemployment and inflation, says the theory, move in opposite directions.

The Federal Reserve always has its ears cocked for issues that concern Congress and the press. When high unemployment attracts attention, the Fed draws down short-term interest rates in an effort to speed up the economy. This may increase inflation modestly, but it reduces unemployment.

Alternatively, when high inflation attracts attention, the Fed increases short-term rates, allowing unemployment to increase modestly but reducing inflation.

The Phillips Curve theory, however, is bogus. Sometimes unemployment and inflation move together. During the 1970s, for example, the word "stagflation" came to the fore. Even though the economy was stagnating and high unemployment prevailed, inflation was also high. Did the Fed discard the theory?

Not on your life. Discarding the theory would have meant the Fed should do less. It would have to reduce its interference in the economy. Can't have that. Perhaps they assumed that the 1970s experience was just an aberration.

Then came 2018 and 2019, after corporate tax rates were reduced and destructive regulations were cancelled. The economy was strong, and unemployment was at rock bottom. But inflation was low as well. This time, the Fed acknowledged that unemployment and inflation had moved in the same direction. But the Fed did not say that the Phillips Curve theory is bogus. Admitting this would imply that the Fed should allow the economy to correct itself, an implication that would not fit the needs of Federal Reserve employees.

The statement currently at the beginning of the Federal Reserve website reads, "As the Federal Reserve conducts monetary policy, it influences employment and inflation primarily through the use of its policy tools to influence the availability and cost of credit in the economy."

This statement indicates the Fed, unfortunately, will remain active in its monetary management. Also, linking employment and inflation so closely together at the very beginning of the website reveals that Mr. Phillips, who died in 1975, remains alive and well in the minds of Federal Reserve employees.

Two Percent Inflation

On November 16, 1977, Congress amended the Federal Reserve Act, requiring the Board "to promote effectively the goals of maximum employment, stable prices, and moderate long-term interest rates."

(Congress seems unaware that the only long-term goal any central bank can achieve is price stability. Any other endeavor causes more problems than it solves.)

"Stable prices" implies that prices should remain level, wouldn't you agree?

The Fed does not agree. This may be a standard too difficult for the Fed to achieve. It might be subject to blame. The Fed therefore gives itself an out. It sets a target for its core inflation rate at 2% a year. (The "core" rate strips out volatile food and gasoline prices.) Even though Congress may not have intended this change, it seems to have accepted it.

Although the Fed has *set* a goal of 2% inflation, fortunately it has not achieved it of late. The economy in 2019 and early-2020 was strong, with low unemployment, low interest rates, and low inflation. At the time, the Fed created enormous amounts of new money. The primary purpose was to achieve lower interest rates. Low rates the Fed did achieve. Inflation of 2% it did not, about which the Fed has expressed regret.

Inflation of 2% a year would cause the value of the nation's savings to fall by half in 35 years—less than two generations. Would this contribute to a healthy economy? No. America is better off with no inflation.

On Aug. 27, 2020, the Fed announced it would tolerate inflation above 2% in the short term if this maximized employment. Instead of 2% inflation being a ceiling, the Fed made it an *average* objective. So much for stable prices. The Fed wants to continue exercising power.

Errors during the Great Depression

The Great Depression was an economic disaster. Lasting a decade, industrial production plummeted, unemployment soared, and people suffered terribly. The depression spread around the globe, the longest and deepest downturn in modern times.

On November 8, 2002, Ben Bernanke, then a member of the Federal Reserve Board of Governors, said in a speech regarding the Great Depression, "We did it, we're very sorry, and we won't do it again."

He was referring to several Fed policies during the Great Depression that he considered errant, as follows:

1. The Fed raised interest rates rapidly in 1928 and 1929 in an attempt to limit speculation in securities markets. The rapid pace of advance slowed economic activity sharply. The increase in rates, Mr. Bernanke believes, should have begun earlier and been more gradual.

2. The Fed failed to act as a lender of last resort during the banking panics that extended from 1930 to 1933. It should have created money to alleviate the pain.

3. It failed to stem the 30% decline in the supply of money from

1930 to 1933, which resulted from the collapse of the banking system. Average prices and wages declined by 30%. In 1933, unemployment reached 25.6%. Debt burdens proliferated. Numerous businesses were forced into bankruptcy, all of which the Fed could have lessened by significantly increasing the money supply.

No doubt the above solutions would have reduced the economic problems, and Mr. Bernanke has promised not to make such errors again. But he omitted a vital factor: The Great Depression was caused, lengthened, and intensified mostly by Presidents Herbert Hoover, Franklin Roosevelt and the Congresses, not the Fed. Evidently Mr. Bernanke may be unable to see beyond the confines of his own institution

President Hoover was an enormously capable engineer and administrator who set out to "engineer" an improved economy. In the year of his inauguration, 1929, he proposed to increase agricultural tariffs to help American farmers, who were indeed in trouble. Partly because of earlier government policies that had helped farmers increase production and because of improved agricultural technology, agricultural prices had at first advanced smartly. But farm surpluses the government had helped the farmers achieve, together with the revival of farming in Europe after World War I, then caused agricultural prices to plummet. The least damaging policy would have been for the U.S. government not to have encouraged the earlier growth and not to try to prevent the later bankruptcies. Farmers would have been better off if the government had done nothing throughout. The initial upside and the subsequent downside would both have been reduced.

But no, Mr. Hoover and the Congress wanted action. Tariffs on agricultural imports were increased substantially. On Black Monday, October 28, 1929, the U.S. stock market plummeted in waves. Why? Because a succession of reports from the Capital were telegraphed to Wall Street as votes were taken by a Congressional committee, applying high tariffs, not just to farming, but to a wide range of industrial products. Stock traders recognized that the high and broadly applied tariffs in the Smoot-Hawley Bill, which passed in 1930, would have a devastating impact on the U.S. economy.

President Hoover also wanted additional government revenues to set up agencies to engineer a better economy, and he asked for significantly higher income tax rates. This was accomplished in 1932, raising the top tax rate from 25% to 63%. President Franklin Roosevelt followed up with numerous ill-advised policies that intensified and lengthened the Great Depression.

Had the entire government done nothing about the economy in the 1920s and 1930s, there would probably have been a modest decline because bankers had forgotten how to evaluate loans correctly during the gangbuster economic growth in the 1920s.[8] The agony of the Great Depression was caused primarily by the government and the Federal Reserve Bank.

The best way for the government to be helpful is to stop being helpful. Mr. Bernanke clearly does not know this. Doing nothing, with low, flat tax rates, does not meet the needs of government employees. When an obvious economic problem arises, government bureaucrats want to repair it. It does not occur to them that the problem would be milder and would repair itself more quickly if the economy had been controlled all along by free markets and not by government.

Misinterpretation of Low Interest Rates

The Federal Reserve Bank, especially the man who later became its chairman, Paul Bernanke, has been too preoccupied with the Great Depression. In the 1930s, low interest rates were caused by grave economic weakness. Low interest rates, however, sometimes result from a strong economy, which produces so much in the way of goods

---

8. *E. C. Harwood, a Biographical Sketch of the Founder of the American Institute for Economic Research,* by Katy Delay, AIER, 2018.

and services that they outrun the availability of money, causing prices and interest rates to fall. Such has been the case in Switzerland more than anywhere else.

In 2018 and 2019, this occurred also in the United States. President Trump's reduction of corporate tax rates and cancellation of numerous regulations that had throttled industrial production provided a huge thrust to the economy. So much production occurred that industrial prices and interest rates fell. The Federal Reserve Bank mistakenly interpreted these as economic weakness, as they certainly had been in the 1930s. The Fed therefore created a substantial amount of new money, supposedly to correct the weakness.

But the economy was not weak. It was forging ahead. The unnecessary new money simply laid the groundwork for higher inflation. The Fed prefers not to take account of any such strength because this would imply that the Fed should do nothing except create new money at rates that enable prices to remain level. Doing so little is anathema to government employees. It deprives them of the opportunity to exercise power.

Keynesian Economics

Lord John Maynard Keynes, who died in 1946, was a brilliant man. It was said that on one day he could convince a person of a certain economic argument. The next day, he could convince the same person with equal clarity and veracity of the very opposite economic argument.

Some economists and politicians favor helping the economy's supply side. Ronald Reagan and Donald Trump both supported this approach. They believed correctly that if the government reduced income tax rates and cancelled regulations that impeded production, the economy would thrive, with millions of workers hired.

Other economists and politicians favor helping the economy's demand side. Franklin Roosevelt, Lyndon Johnson, and Richard Nixon supported this approach. (On one occasion, Mr. Nixon said, "We're all Keynesians now.") They suggest providing government money to the people, who would then demand products to get the economy rolling.

Maynard Keynes came down on both sides. But since his main work took place during the 1920s and 1930s, when world economies had been weakened by war, he tended at the time, probably mistakenly, to favor the demand side. His followers, most of them less brilliant than he, have favored helping the demand side all the time, and they do so with more enthusiasm than Mr. Keynes would likely have entertained.

Why is this so? Because helping the demand side provides more work for government bureaucrats and economists. This group here needs extra money. That group there needs extra money. Another group over there, no, they already have the resources they need. Cash for payouts must be found. Tax rates must be raised. There's plenty for economists and politicians to do to bolster the demand side.

Not so for the supply side. Yes, tax rates need to be cut, but that's a one-shot deal. Damaging regulations need to be cancelled but, for the most part, this simply requires numerous presidential signatures. Everyone can then sit back and watch the economy take off.

Bureaucrats are uncomfortable sitting back and watching. This implies that people in the private sector, without the use of force, can exercise economic power in free markets. Heavens, they might make mistakes! Government bureaucrats are empowered to exercise real force, and they darn well like to do so. After all, they're government, and they don't make mistakes, right?

Whatever the Fed and the government choose to do now will almost certainly be wrong. The Fed has followed various misconceptions for years, just as the Soviet Union followed five-year plans that couldn't help but fail.

The economy has no plan and no goals. It simply adjusts for

changes in every cubic millimeter of space, nature, and things. It adjusts for changes in the character, inclinations, and capabilities of every person. It adjusts everywhere, during every millisecond of time. Lumbering central planning can do nothing except disrupt, leaving everyone worse off.

Except for government employees. No matter what happens, they are seldom worse off.

ONWARD AND DOWNWARD WITH QE[9]

In a webcast on January 14, 2021, Fed Chairman Jerome Powell said, "Now is not the time to exit" from easy money policies. "The economy is far from our goals."

Every month since June 2020, the Fed has bought $80 billion of Treasury securities and $40 billion of mortgage bonds. These purchases are called "quantitative easing." The QEs will continue until the Fed sees "substantial further progress" in the job market.

$80 billion Treasury securities and $40 billion mortgage bonds total $120 billion a month. Multiplying by 6 months, from June 2020 to the present, gives a total of $720 billion, much of which will add to the national debt.

$720 billion. The defense of the United States, with its 2.76 million warriors and civilian employees, costs $740 billion this year. In only six months, the nine brawny members of the Federal Reserve's Board of Governors have passed out almost as much money as was needed for the nation's defense in an entire year. They did this all by themselves. Now those are *real* warriors.

The Fed has pushed short-term interest rates to near zero and has said it expects to keep them low for years.

During the 2007-2009 Credit Crisis, the Fed did a great deal of

---

9. WSJ, Jon Hilsenrath, *Powell Hints at More Easy-Money Policy,* 1/15/21.

quantitative easing. Yet the U.S. suffered the slowest emergence from that crisis of any recession in memory. Powell blamed the slow recovery from the Credit Crisis on insufficient deficit spending by the U.S. government. Way to go, Jerome. When what you're doing doesn't work, blame someone else.

Quantitative easing never works. Neither do the one-time stimulus checks to individuals or businesses. In 2009, Congress passed an $800 billion stimulus bill to revitalize the economy and reduce unemployment. Neither purpose was accomplished, because businesses do not invest and endeavor to grow based on a one-time source of revenue.

Gerald Ford, Jimmy Carter, George W. Bush, and Barack Obama all passed out freebies. According to a large-scale study by the National Bureau of Economic Research, "Most respondents report that they primarily saved or paid down debts with their transfers, with only about 15 percent reporting that they mostly spent it."[10]

Grants from the federal government to state and local governments have also been unnecessary. They simply cut back spending their own money and used the federal money instead.

Studies have found that peoples' consumption is generally determined, not by government freebies, but by the income they expect to have over the long term. This seems sensible to me.

Additional studies have determined that economic growth improves when limits are placed on the growth of federal spending. Ditto.

But of course we want to give the members of the Federal Reserve Board of Governors something to do. We want them to be happy in their work. We don't pay them to figure out how to repay the national debt. We pay them to add to it. They won't be personally held responsible when they're wrong. Why, it's shocking to even *think* of such a thing!

---

10. WSJ, John F. Cogan and John B. Taylor, *Those $2,000 Checks Won't Boost the Economy*, 1/15/21.

But hasn't the amount of money added to the debt been gargantuan? Doesn't matter. We owe it to ourselves.

SHADOW BANKING IS HUGE

Andy Kessler, former venture capitalist and hedge-fund manager, is now a columnist for the Wall Street Journal. His column on January 4, 2021 described the new era of "shadow banking."[11]

To understand how shadow banking works now, first understand how banking worked before, and still does to a limited extent:

Let's say the Fed creates money out of nothing and gives or loans it to you by crediting your bank account.

Your bank loans a goodly portion of the new deposit to Party B. This is also new money.

Party B deposits that money in her bank, which then lends part of it to Party C.

On it goes, with each bank lending a goodly portion of the last person's new money. Each subsequent loan is smaller and smaller, until finally the last penny is lent. That's it, until the Fed starts another round, which it's likely to do in about three minutes.

Banks create money. This is legal. It's been going on for hundreds of years. Without it, all economies would be up the creek.

Before computers, the money creations left paper trails. The system could operate only as long as the banks could write, and later type, on all that paper.

Enter the new day: No paper. The new money is electronic. The loans are electronic. Even Treasury securities are electronic. Well, maybe you can get a Savings Bonds on embossed paper to give to your grandchildren. But most Treasuries are not paperized. (New word. You have to be really special to create a new word.) The Treasuries are carefully identified with letters and numbers, but they exist only

---

11. WSJ, Andy Kessler, *How the Fed Stifles Lending,* 1/3/21.

in electronic form.

The sequence of loans described above is based on fractions of the money initially created by the Fed. This is now true for only 15% or less of current loans. Most loans today do not begin with money creations by the Fed. They begin and end with the world's banks, money markets, asset managers, broker-dealers, hedge funds, and other companies that deal with money, all apart from the Fed. It's a stupendous amount of lending, mostly based on very short-term loans, and it's called "shadow banking."

Among other things, shadow banking supports the global supply chains that bring goods cheaply from throughout the world to stores like Walmart, Amazon, and others.

Here's how shadow banking works. Financial Institution A obtains a loan lasting from one day to a week from Financial Institution B. As collateral, A provides a short-term Treasury Bill (called a "T-Bill"). A also promises to pay a little extra to B when the loan matures up to a week later. The whole thing is called a Repo Loan, meaning "Repurchase Agreement." The little extra, specified in advance, constitutes the rate of interest on the loan. If A is unable to repay the loan, which happens rarely, B keeps the collateral. Sometimes the collateral offered is riskier than Treasuries, but usually T-Bills serve as the collateral.

When they're first sold, T-Bills have maturities of 4, 8, 13, 26, and 52 weeks. It doesn't matter that the maturities are longer than the Repo Loans.

Here's where shadow banking becomes intriguing: Financial Institution A gave a T-Bill to B as collateral for a loan. B is now in possession of collateral she didn't have before. She therefore offers the same T-Bill to C in return for another short-term loan. That is also new money.

C offers the same collateral to D. D offers it to E, and finally E to

H, making up to eight successive loans, all secured by that same poor little T-Bill.

Upon maturity all the loans are repaid, with new loans offered. That T-Bill served as collateral for loans totaling many times its value. Collectively, the loans are used to pay Asians to make stuff and pay for humongous container ships to carry it across the Pacific.

Does all this sound risky to you?

Me too.

We're talking billions of dollars of loans to fund massive amounts of trades. Each loan, just a few days long, is backed up by a short-term Treasury Bill. But each of those Treasury Bills backs up a *succession* of loans. As a whole, the loans are therefore significantly under-collateralized. It's like a huge building carefully constructed with playing cards.

The passing of collateral from one party to the next is called "rehypothecation." Drop that word at your next social gathering to show how cool you are. Stress the syllables "ree," "poth," and especially "cay," and the word will flow off your tongue like you've been using it since you were in kindergarten.

"These transfers," Andy Kessler writes, "used to be done once or twice for each posted asset, but are now sometimes done six to eight times, each time creating new money supply. All this money creation is outside the purview of the Federal Reserve—and it's huge."

There have been few defaults so far, and the system enables tremendous savings for Americans, because an enormous amount of money for fairly long-term use is based on very short-term loans whose risks are low and whose interest rates are historically low.

Yes, the system worked ... until the various loan participants ran out of collateral. In March 2020, the shadow-banking system did almost run out of collateral, because the Fed had gobbled up enormous numbers of T-Bills with its quantitative easing.

(Beginning with the 2008 Credit Crisis and again with the 2020 lockdown crisis, the Fed engaged in trillions of dollars of loans, mostly to banks, in what they called quantitative easing, supposedly to ease America's financial strain. Money goes out to the banks. Treasury securities, short and long term, transfer to the Fed and electronically disappear.)

But the shadow bankers needed those dear little T-Bills as collateral for their loans. Their disappearance was a problem, as a result of which the interest rates on the badly needed T-Bills went haywire in March 2020.

But Congress came along just in time with the Cares Act, under which the government passed out $1,200 checks and other funds for payroll protection, bailouts, and unemployment bonuses. To provide the funds, the Treasury Department auctioned off $2 trillion of new debt, including T-Bills—just what the shadow bankers needed.

To prevent the shortage from happening again, Kessler suggested that the Fed discontinue quantitative easing and stop buying up T-Bills. With plentiful collateral available, the rehypothecation could take place 2-3 times, not 6-8 times, reducing the risk.

A few general observations:

- The use of extremely short-term money for long-term loans reflects the high risk of the current economy.

- The high risk justifies the title of this book.

- The capacity of shadow banking to create amounts of money even greater than that created by the Fed carries the potential for inflation and thus considerably higher interest rates.

THE FED BLOWS IT AGAIN

Beginning with the Credit Crisis in 2008, the Federal Reserve Bank bought a significant amount of Treasury bonds and notes from banks and other members of the public, paying for them with money created out of nothing. "Quantitative Easing" was the name. Its purpose was to lessen the economic pain of the crisis.

In March 2020, for the first time in history, the Fed began buying bonds that had been issued by *corporations*. The purpose was to sustain the operations of the companies and keep employees on the payroll.

The Fed's buying of corporate debt was unnecessary. By the end of March, disruptions in the corporate debt market had largely dissipated. In fact, during the difficult early months of 2020, large companies raised more money from private lenders than they'd raised during the early months of 2019. For large companies, there was no shortage of liquidity.

Buying corporate bonds by the Fed may have done more harm than good, for the following reasons:

- In buying the bonds indiscriminately, the Fed relieved the debt of companies that were in a position to grant huge executive compensations or shareholder distributions.

- The purchase of corporate bonds failed to relieve the debt of companies that had significant numbers of U.S. workers. From March to September 2020, companies that had benefited from the Fed's largesse nevertheless laid off more than a million workers. Boeing laid off 16,000 employees. Sysco laid off a third of its workforce, while continuing to pay its shareholders a dividend.

- Companies too small to have borrowed from the public by issuing corporate bonds received nothing from the Fed's purchases. They had no bonds available for purchase.

- The Fed purchased the debt of "fallen angels," i.e., bonds that had fallen to junk status. In other words, companies that had over-borrowed were rewarded with free cash, while companies frugal enough to avoid over-borrowing were disregarded.

- Small companies are the primary source of job creation and innovation in America. They were not helped by the purchase of corporate bonds because they had none to sell. Large companies were indeed helped by the sale of their bonds, and they used the money to buy smaller competitors. Those ex-competitors, thus absorbed by the larger corporations, were no longer in a position to do as much hiring and innovating.

- The Fed's bailouts were a windfall for large companies and their investors.

- The huge and unnecessary bailout of corporate debt also benefited the Wall Street underwriters of debt issues, an indirect form of crony capitalism.

- Passing out enormous amounts of new money with the Fed's quantitative easing also laid a foundation for the eventual resurgence of inflation.[12]

Since government agencies make no profits by which workers can measure their self-esteem, they measure their self-esteem by actively exercising power, such as the Fed's buying of corporate bonds. The state and city lockdowns, having caused massive economic problems, provided an opportunity for the Fed to leap into the breach and exercise power galore, probably making the long-term economic problems worse.

Adverse long-term consequences? Never mind; the Fed can look at those later. Besides, adverse long-term consequences would provide

---

12. WSJ, Sheila Bair and Lawrence Goodman, *Corporate Debt 'Relief' is an Economic Dud*, 1/7/21.

an opportunity to take all the more action in the future.

The Federal Reserve Bank continues to cause tremendous harm to the U.S. economy. One failure after another. Is it not obvious that the nation would be better off relying on free-market capitalism to allocate its resources, not top-down control?

The nation's monetary system should be delegated to the people, as described in Chapter 2. The Federal Reserve System should be relegated to its inglorious history and abolished.

CHAPTER 4
The Hijacked Election of 2020

WHY THE MEDIA IS SO LIBERAL

WHY ARE THE PEOPLE WHO work in media so far out on the left?

They don't realize it, but it's in their financial interest to be on the left. The left is government. The right is free markets.

(The numerous Republicans-in-Name-Only (RINOs) in Congress proclaim they're on the right. But they're pretty closely allied with the true liberals. The RINOs probably think it's possible to go over the cliff a little more slowly. Lots of luck with that.)

Free markets are boring. What 328 million people are doing individually, going about the business of living, is seldom high drama. When sex, wrongdoing, or pathos are involved, fine, the media can jump on those. But stories and shows about humdrum things happening in the private sector usually attract little interest and have low advertising rates. A woman takes her kid to school and goes to work? Not exactly earthshaking. So-and-so is the new CEO of a company? Unless he's already in the public eye, who cares?

Government is a different story. It can exert force. What government does often affects everyone. This does indeed attract viewer interest and has high advertising rates.

For the media, government means money. Media moguls don't even want to contemplate that government in the long run does more harm than good. They prefer to believe that government is a source of good and hire people who agree.

Young college graduates entering the news business want to make society better. They have not been taught that government generally makes it worse.

The media has a huge conflict of interest that people in media are unaware of. What brings in the most money to them creates harm for the people.

Major newspapers and television networks are no longer in the news business. They're in politics. They endeavor to persuade readers and viewers to vote Democratic. They omit bad news about Democrats and omit good news about conservative Republicans.

Magazine cover stories about first ladies have always been common. Yet, during the four years of the Trump administration, not a single cover story appeared about the woman who seemed to me the most beautiful and exquisitely dressed first lady in American history.

The Wall Street Journal, Fox News, Newsmax, and Citizen Free Press do a good job of it.

But surprisingly, the WSJ seems unaware, or chooses not to become aware, of the corruption in the 2020 presidential election. It maintains that the rejection of cases by the courts was evidence that the corruption didn't happen.

It did happen. Mr. Trump lacked focus and chose the wrong people to represent him on the issue. Some of the courts, having been controlled by Democrats for decades, found it easy to declare that the cases lacked standing. Other judges may have been never-Trumpers. Unfortunately, the reporting on the voting machines, which were the most consequential source of cheating, has been minimal.

MAN BEHIND THE SCENE

December 7, 2020. During the last four years, Democratic efforts were coordinated by a canny political operator from behind the scene.

To draw attention away from Hillary Clinton transferring secret documents to her private server, the man advised the Democrats, FBI, CIA, and the press to concoct the notion that the Russians had arranged Trump's victory. He suggested this despite former President Obama having said that U.S. presidential politics are too complicated and diverse for a foreign government to determine a particular outcome.

The man arranged for well-respected Representative Jim Clyburn to back Joe Biden, putting Biden over the top in the primaries. But with Biden's presidential capacity dubious, the man chose as vice president his favorite senator, Kamala Harris, the Senate's most liberal member.

To assure Biden's victory, Democrats needed to cheat big time in just seven counties, where Democrats controlled the local governments, police departments, and the courts. Carry Philadelphia, Pittsburg, Minneapolis, Detroit, Las Vegas, Milwaukee, and Atlanta, and Biden would become president.

The voting machines had been prepared with algorithms that anticipated a Trump plurality, which could be surreptitiously overcome. But the algorithms didn't anticipate a Trump landslide. After the polls closed on election night, the man told the seven counties to stop counting until extraordinary measures were taken. (At least within the view of Republican observers, all seven counties quit counting at the same time. These underground activities were clearly coordinated.)

Huge numbers of fake ballots were supplied. Most importantly, persons abroad, including in China, used their internet access to individual voting machines to reprogram them and shift votes from Trump to Biden.

Only one person I know of has the savvy, stature, and lying ability to carry this off: Barack (don't tell anyone I'm a committed socialist) Obama.

I heard Mr. Biden say on television on December 4 that he had told Obama that if he and Kamala Harris have a moral disagreement, he, Biden, would "develop some disease" and resign. It seemed like Biden was talking to the boss. Biden is just the placeholder. Kamala Harris is Obama's choice for president.

Whether you like it or not.

HILLARY'S BRIBE

December 21, 2020. Patrick M. Byrne has been a leader of various fledgling companies and was the founder and CEO of Overstock.com. More information about him is available in Wikipedia.

In a 5-minute video shown by Citizen Free Press, Mr. Byrne disclosed that he was asked by the FBI to meet secretly with Hillary Clinton on January 14, 2016. During the meeting, Byrne gave her a check for $18 million, which had been supplied by Turkey in anticipation of Hillary being elected president in November 2016.

Delivery of the check was arranged by President Obama for the purpose of holding Hillary accountable. Other than the few people involved in the meeting, no one was to know about the bribe. But if Clinton, as president, undermined Obama's precious Obamacare, the bribe would be disclosed, and she'd be in serious legal trouble.

Obama also planned that after Hillary had served as president for eight years, Michelle Obama would succeed her.

Obama had placed his people throughout the bureaucracies, especially the Justice Department. William Barr, later the U.S. attorney general, knew about the bribe.

Trump's victory in 2016 was a surprise. Obama then directed that

Trump should be accused of Russian collusion, a pure fabrication.

Two years later, in 2018, Byrne was assured by the FBI that Donald Trump's reelection bid in 2020 would be "hijacked."

By April 2021, Mr. Byrne's video had been pulled. But it was forthright and detailed. I believe Patrick Byrne told the truth.

TRUMP LOST ONLY BECAUSE OF CHEATING

November 9, 2020. Sorry, Associated Press, the Constitution does not authorize you to certify who is president.

President Trump would have won reelection except for the cheating of vote-counting in states led by Democrats.

The cheating should be challenged in court, and Mr. Trump should dispassionately explain why the challenge is necessary.

"Count every vote" is wrong. The correct dictum: Count every *legal* vote.

It may be too late. I doubt that the ballots are being held under Republican surveillance 24 hours a day. If not, ballots can readily be destroyed to make Biden the winner.

If the holding of ballots has not been under 24-hour Republican surveillance and if the lawsuits do not succeed, the elections in those Democratic-run states should be undertaken again, with inauguration postponed as long as necessary. I'm not holding my breath in anticipation.

(February 2021. Immediately after the November election, I was unaware of the corruption of the voting machines. This was a crucial factor in the election. It must be addressed and corrected.)

BIG LOSSES FOR DEMOCRATS IN 2020

Except for the few states that swung the 2020 presidential election for Biden, Democrats suffered heavy losses throughout America.

President Trump had a landslide victory, but lost his election because of opposition cheating. Without the corruption, Michigan Republican John James would have replaced a Democrat in the U.S. Senate.

In various videos, Sidney Powell and Rudi Giuliani explained how the presidency was stolen. A video of an 8-minute television appearance by Sidney Powell was no longer available when this book went to press. It described in great detail the extent of corruption in the seven cities that swung the election from Trump to Biden, especially the corruption of the voting machines.

State legislatures must be held accountable to repair election laws and practices. They certainly should trash those crooked machines.

In other than the seven corrupt counties, the Republicans won handily. Speaker Pelosi expected to gain 10 to 12 seats in the House. Instead, she lost 9.

Hundreds of millions of dollars were paid by Michael Bloomberg, George Soros, Mark Zuckerberg, and others to help Democrats control state legislatures. The people voted Republican anyway, gaining 192 members in state houses and 40 members in state senates.

In 23 states, Republicans now control both legislative bodies and the governorship (called "trifectas"). Democrat trifectas prevail in 15 states, divided governments in only 12.

It was a blue wave, right? Yes, providing you're color blind.

TIME LINE

January 15, 2021. On the infamous day the Capital building was breached, January 6, 2021, the supposed instigator, Donald Trump, began his speech at the Eclipse at noon and ended it at 1:11 p.m. It was only at the end that he urged his followers to march on the capital and peacefully carry out a demonstration. (He did say "peacefully.")

Cell phones were unusable in the area that day, and no vehicles were allowed in the vicinity. From the Eclipse to the Capital was a 45-minute walk. Without being marathon runners, the earliest that people could have arrived at the Capital after hearing the end of the speech was about 1:56 p.m.

Then they could begin breaching the Capital, right?

Well, no. The Capital had already been breached. This occurred at 12:55, about an hour before anyone hearing the end of the President's speech could have gotten there. A relatively small group had already gathered at the Capital.

That small group must have been set up by Trump. After all, Congress has impeached him for causing the attack, and Congress is always right.

Right?

INAUGURATION

January 25, 2021. If the Democrats had allowed regular folks to attend the inauguration, there would probably have been booing. This having little appeal to the Democrats, they filled the spaces with hundreds of thousands of flags, allowing only their supporters to witness the ceremony.

On his first day in office, President Biden canceled the Keystone XL pipeline, making the environmentalists happy, but keeping some 10,000 workers from good-paying jobs and giving Canada the cold shoulder.

Due to puppet-master Barack Obama, it may not be long before Kamala Harris steps in as our next president.

Besides raising tax rates, here are some of the Biden/Harris policy plans:

- End Right-to-Work Laws: Millions of workers will be forced to join unions, paying union dues whether they like it or not.

- End America's Energy Independence: They'll ban the use of fossil fuels, probably by 2035. No thought of encouraging fracking, which produces natural gas that's very low on CO_2. No thought of lifting unnecessary regulations on nuclear power plants that generate electricity efficiently with no CO_2. No thought of capturing a small amount of the sun's energy with solar collectors in space and beaming it to earth. Exercising force on people is more fun. Better to ban the use of fossil fuels and substitute renewable fuels. These are many times more expensive, because the sun doesn't shine and the wind doesn't blow all the time, and the amount of land needed for these purposes is huge. The economy would be ruined, hurting the poor most. Environmentalists prefer that you not notice the millions of birds that would be killed by those towering whirling blades on land and sea.

- Bail out deadbeat states like California, Illinois, New Jersey, and New York with $400 billion as a reward for their profligacy.

- Increase the minimum wage to $15 an hour: This will put many small businesses out of business. It will force many employees to change from full-time to part-time work. The number of people who find jobs at below the minimum wage will greatly outnumber those who benefit from the higher minimum wage.

Way to go, Joe and Kamala. You'll be doing your bit to make life harder for the poor and the environment.

President Bill Clinton went overboard with socialism in his first two years, causing the Congressional election that followed to swing big time to Republicans. President Obama went overboard with socialism early in his administration, causing another big Congressional swing toward conservativism. I expect Presidents Biden, Harris, and the Congressional socialists to go overboard now. One hopes they will be overthrown in the elections of 2022 and thereafter, perhaps even permanently.

In the meantime, there's danger. The liberal elite includes the heads of large, technically competent corporations and the media. If you cast aspersions on big government, they're coming after you. You'll be considered a white supremacist no matter what color you are. They'll want you to shut your mouth and keep it shut. The social media crowd and their enforcement goons will cut you off. For more extreme measures, Black Lives Matter and Antifa may get the nod.

WHY PEOPLE VOTED FOR TRUMP

November 15, 2020. Some political experts think that many lower-income Democrats voted for Trump because his style reminded them of themselves and their local Democrat politicians.

The analysis is incomplete. Most voters intuit that it's the *policies* that count, not the mannerisms.

Ronald Reagan, who was better prepared for the presidency even than Woodrow Wilson, didn't remind Democratic voters of themselves or their local politicians. They just sensed that Reagan's policies were correct.

Richard Nixon, the most awkward candidate ever to run for president, didn't remind voters of anyone. The people simply preferred his policies.

Intuition has a larger role in politics than the experts think. Both Trump and Reagan attracted numerous Democrats because voters sensed intuitively that they were right. The only reason Trump lost in 2020 was because of electoral cheating.

Dear Reader,

Part of the laudatory blurb on the back cover of this book reads, "Except for one satirical piece, the line of understanding never breaks."

This is the piece. In a few places, it's hard to tell what's satirical and what isn't. Best to stay on the ball. But it doesn't matter if you don't. No one's going to test you.

— Archie

THE RECORD OF THAT WRETCHED, INCOMPETENT DONALD TRUMP

January 18, 2021. In the end, Trump's sensitivity and narcissism did him in. It's just as well. He left behind a terrible record of public policies, right? It's no wonder that the liberal elite hated him. Here's a partial list:

- Trump foolishly raised tariffs, disrupting normal international trade. All presidents should know that in every trade, both parties benefit. Anyone not benefiting would not make the trade to begin with. Also, the United States has had trade deficits during most of its history, but the nation thrived nevertheless. Every effort should be made to cut tariffs, not raise them.

- For far too long, Trump gave his support to Anthony Fauci and Deborah Birx. Their outrageous mortality projections scared Americans half to death, paving the way for the disastrous and unnecessary lockdowns. Trump should have pitted Fauci one on one against an epidemiologist of an opposing view, like John Ioannidis of Stanford, or Martin Kulldorff of Harvard. Fauci would almost certainly have lost the debate, in which case he should have been excluded thereafter from entering the White House.

- Trump simplified the tax code and cut corporate tax rates significantly. Everybody knows that's dumb.

- He cancelled numerous Obama regulations that were throttling production. Imagine cancelling well-meaning regulations by our beloved President Obama!

- The cut in tax rates and the cancelling of regulations boosted the economy to all-time new highs. They also elevated black employment to new highs, with black poverty and unemployment rates the lowest ever recorded. Aren't blacks supposed to remain poor, making them more likely to respond with their votes when Democrats promise to help them?

- Trump appointed 239 federal judges, including three to the Supreme Court. They're constitutionalist, meaning the judge interprets the ordinary meaning of the legal text, even if he or she doesn't agree with the law.

- He improved the Veterans Administration dramatically.

- Arranged long-overdue maintenance and improvements to the national parks.

- Signed a law that makes cruelty to animals a felony.

- Signed right-to-try legislation, allowing terminally ill patients to try experimental treatments.

- Signed the First Step Act, which freed mostly black prisoners from unfair sentences, expanded opportunities for the rehabilitation of prisoners, and ended the "three-strikes" provision. The Act reformed sentencing laws to cut recidivism and reduce federal inmate populations.

- Approved drilling for oil in the Arctic National Wildlife Refuge, occupying for that purpose a microscopic percentage of its 19.6 million acreage.

- Combatted anti-Semitism on college campuses.

- Stopped kangaroo courts on campuses that accused male students of sexual assaults without permitting them to cross-examine their accusers. (Leftists believe women who accuse men of sexual abuse should not be challenged. The women can be challenged, however, when Joe Biden is one of the accused.)

- Despite fervent opposition from teachers' unions, Trump promoted charter schools and vouchers for private schools.

- Trump repealed the Obama rule that cut off aid for vocational programs of schools run for profit.

- Ruled that federal bureaucrats cancel two regulations for every new regulation imposed.

- Enabled bureaucrats to be fired more easily. Previously, it took 6-12 months to remove a poor-performing bureaucrat and another 8 months to resolve appeals, with the individual being paid all along.

- Prevented bureaucrats from being paid for their professional work when spending full time on union activities.

- Withdrew America from the Paris Climate Accord, which has had zero impact in reducing atmospheric CO2, but was costing the United States considerable money.

- Withdrew America from the Iranian nuclear deal, which had not impeded Iran's development of atomic weapons. President Obama had given Iran a minimum of $50 billion of "useable liquid assets" that had been frozen because of previous sanctions against Iran. The payments included $1.7 billion of green cash to release three Americans Iran had imprisoned. Green U.S. cash comes in very handy for terrorist operations.

- Recognized Jerusalem as Israel's capital and moved the U.S. Embassy to Jerusalem.

- Cut off aid to the Palestinian Authority for as long as it paid support to the families of terrorists.

- Set up major diplomatic agreements between Israel and an increasing number of Arab nations. (The dramatic-looking but usually wrong John Kerry: "No, no, no, and no, there will be no separate peace between Israel and Arab nations without resolving the long-standing conflict over Palestine.") Middle East peace, now growing without such a resolution, will almost certainly improve the lives of the Palestinians.

- Rebuilt the U.S. military.

- Created the United States Space Force.

- Focused the world's attention on China's imperial ambitions.

- Killed ISIS terrorist leader Abu Bakr al-Baghdadi and Iran terrorist leader Qasem Soleimani and launched air strikes against Syrian dictator Bashar al-Assad for using chemical weapons. Trump otherwise reduced U.S. military presence in the Mideast.

- Donald Trump was so incompetent that he failed to take advantage of the office he held to increase his own wealth, as do so many members of Congress, not to mention, a recent vice president. According to Forbes, Trump's net worth declined from $3.7 billion in 2016 to $2.5 billion in 2019. This didn't leave the man poverty-stricken, of course, but the decline was 32%. Forebodingly, the 2020 lockdowns have hit hotels, office buildings, and golf courses hard. Normal leverage on real estate can be devastating under such circumstances.

Mr. Trump planned in his second term to reduce individual tax rates and launch another round of economic growth. How foolish can you get? Aren't you glad he lost?

CHAPTER 5
How Government Hurts the Poor

JULIA

PRESIDENT OBAMA'S POLITICAL ADS DURING his 2012 reelection campaign portrayed a fictional woman named Julia, whom government took care of from cradle to grave.

We pose another fictional person, a level-headed woman of limited means, who also happens to be named Julia. She and her mom have many difficulties unintentionally caused by government.

Child Care

Julia's mom needed a job, and also needed to have Julia taken care of. She looked into placing Julia with a competent woman named Penny who runs a Massachusetts daycare for a living. Julia's mom was aghast that the cost exceeded $18,000—way more than she could afford.

She asked Penny, "Why on earth are the costs so high?"

Penny replied, "How I wish it were otherwise. You wouldn't believe how extensive are the regulations imposed by Massachusetts. They deal with the ratio of staff-to-children, training, hygiene, nursing and healthcare, special services, nutrition, licensing, recordkeeping, security of the home, restraints on the children, touching, licensing, personal policies, board of directors, advisory board, written plans for every possible contingency, my finances, and many other matters.

The bureaucrats working for the state are paid plenty. They pat them-selves on the back about the high level of care they're requiring, which makes them look good. But they couldn't care less about the high costs people who need jobs must pay for it."

Julia's mom was forced to give up the idea of child care for Julia. Even if she got a job, she'd have to buy clothes, pay for transportation, and pay FICA tax on the income.

Government regulations can make child care unobtainable for people who most need it—those of low income.

Schooling

The schools for young children in downtown Boston and other central cities are poor. The teachers are boring. The curriculum is far more concerned with racism and diversity than with helping students become honest and productive citizens. Throughout the nation, the numbers of high-paid administrators have increased considerably faster than the number of students.

The Cato Institute compared the cost of educating U.S. public students from Kindergarten to 12th Grade: In 1970, the cost was $57,602. In 2010, it was almost three times higher, $164,426, and this was in *constant* 2013 dollars. If inflation were taken into account, the differential would have been much greater. Yet, over the 40 years, there was no inflation whatever in student reading scores.[13] Clearly, Americans are not receiving value for their education money. (See Chapter 7 about unions.)

Julia's mom wondered why government owned and operated schools. Everybody assumed that if government doesn't do it, it won't be done. She didn't agree. People own and operate stores and all kinds of services for profit. Why not schools?

---

13. AIER, Daniel J. Mitchell, *Government Schools: More Bureaucracy, Lower Performance, and Higher Costs,* 2/18/21.

Government Lotteries Breed Poverty

Julia is now a young adult and has a job checking out customers in a supermarket. She sees enticing ads for the Massachusetts lottery, saying, "No matter what you do for a living, there's an easier way to make money."

"That sounds great," said Julia, "I'll try it, especially since the money is for education."

Over and over she tried, using money she needed for good nutrition and other necessities. The lottery paid her a little here and there, but far less than she spent on it.

She says to a friend, "You know a lot about stuff, Justin. What's with these lotteries for education?"

"They're a ruse, Julia. They trick you into thinking the lottery is for a good purpose. The money you spend on the lottery doesn't have a note attached, saying 'for education only.' It would make no difference if it did. Money is fungible; one dollar is the same as every other dollar. The Massachusetts Treasury spends the money on whatever they're spending that day. Some is for education. Most of it is not.

"State governments rake in nearly $70 billion a year from lotteries. Lotteries are popular. They enable legislators to avoid blame for raising taxes for education.

"In effect, the lotteries are regressive taxes, raising more money from the poor than from the rich. Plus, they create gambling addictions.

"The money comes mostly from people who think it's going to create a nice return for their future. It will do no such thing. In a $759 million state lottery a few years ago, the chances of winning were 1 out of 292 million.

"1 out of 292 is bad enough. But 1 out of 292 *million* is ridiculous. Lotteries are rigged way against you. On average, one dollar gets back only 52 cents. For government to rig lotteries so much against the poor is a disgrace!

"Do your recreational gambling with private companies, Julia. In the long run, you'll lose your money there, too, but your odds will be better than with the government."

Occupational Licensing

Julia tried to get a job as a hair dresser. There aren't many salons around, and they're all fully staffed. Plus, their services cost an arm and a leg.

When she inquired about working for a salon just to braid hair, she's told, "Sorry, you have to pay for a year's training before you can work here."

"A year's training! I braid my own hair. I know how to do it."

"Sorry. It's a state requirement."

"Justin," asks Julia, "What's the purpose of all that training?"

"The purpose is to limit the number of people working as hairdressers, enabling those who are in the business to charge higher prices. People like you are hit the hardest. You don't have the money for training you don't need, which means you can't get those high-paying jobs. But when you use their services, you have to pay their high prices. Besides, in many cases, the training they insist on is not as helpful as training on the job.

"The lobbying that goes on to sustain occupational licensing is rigged against you. Almost a third of Americans need government permission to do their jobs. The author of a report I read looked at about a hundred low-to-moderate-income occupations and found that, on average, the licenses cost about $200 in fees, required 9 months of training, with the passing of a state-approved examination. Pretty stiff requirements for people who need jobs to get by.

"Few people getting out of prison can afford occupational licensing. What are they supposed to do, go back to crime?

"Even licensing for safety is a bad idea. When people get injured, and the supplier is clearly at fault, the injured should sue to recover their costs and perhaps obtain a modest penalty. But I don't go for million-dollar penalties. Nobody's perfect. Those huge penalties are pushed by tort lawyers to make them tons of money. Big penalties raise the premiums of liability insurance and increase costs for everyone.

"I don't even like government licensing of doctors, nurses, and lawyers. These professionals would still receive education and training. Their capabilities would be certified, not by government, but by various professional groups that are in competition with one another. Let the people decide who provides them with services in a free market economy. Government licensing adds nothing except trouble and costs."

Rent Control

Julia said, "I tried to rent an apartment. The rent was sky-high, completely out of my range. But I heard of a woman in the building who had rented the same apartment for some 25 years. Her rent was at rock bottom. What gives, Justin?"

"It's called rent control. For as long as a person remains in an apartment, the law requires that the rent remain the same. The landlord loses a ton of money on this, because his costs have risen tremendously over the 25 years. When a tenant vacates, the landlord can jack up the rent for newcomers. Without this, he couldn't stay in business. If the government forces him to lose money with some tenants, he has to make it up with others.

"Tenants who remain in an apartment for years may not be superrich, but they tend to be older, their lives are stable, and they have reliable sources of income. The people forced to pay the high rents tend to move a lot. They're generally younger, their lives are not stable, and many do not have reliable sources of income."

"Instead of all that regulation," says Julia, "why don't they just build more apartments?"

"Because of building restrictions."

"Well, then, why not remove the restrictions?"

"Because voters who are relatively prosperous urge their political representatives to impose the restrictions. They resist urbanization. They don't want people they consider riff-raff coming in and supposedly ruining their neighborhood."

"Thanks a lot," says Julia. "I guess I'll have to apply for an apartment intended for the poor."

Housing for the Poor

"Perhaps so," says Justin. "It's a shame that housing for the poor has to be a government program, supported by federal housing subsidies. The apartments are built by private companies. The tenants pay a little less in rents. But their savings don't match the amounts of the government subsidies. No, the major beneficiaries of the subsidies are the companies who build the housing and the people who provide the financing. It's an indirect form of crony capitalism—federal subsidies that benefit the rich.

"If they did away with rent control, zoning laws, and all sorts of government regulations, attractive, multi-family housing projects would be built by free market capitalism. In the long run, everyone would benefit, but especially people of limited means like you. While we're at it, let's close down Housing and Urban Development (HUD), a federal agency with 8,000 employees that spends $40 billion a year and prevents free market capitalism from operating in housing markets."

Minimum Wages

Julia says, "President Biden wants to double minimum wages to $15 an hour. If I can get a minimum wage job, that would be great for me. What do you think about it?"

"I hope you get a minimum wage job, Julia. But the jobs will be hard to get because the extra wage cost makes employers reluctant to hire at the minimum wage. The laws will raise the prices of things and services that are supplied by those who work for minimum wages. The laws will also make companies that are only marginally success-ful to fire their employees and go out of business, reducing the supply of goods and generally increasing prices.

"Most businesses care about their employees. To avoid going bankrupt, they may have to require some of the employees to change from full-time to part-time work, even though the business owner would prefer not to.

"Also, a great many jobs are not subject to minimum wage require-ments. Millions of small businesses with revenues below $500,000 a year that do not engage in interstate commerce are not subject to minimum wage laws. Neither are seasonal farm workers and newspa-per delivery workers. Surprisingly enough, the total number of work-ers paid less than minimum wages outnumber those who are subject to the minimum by about three times.

"Every time the minimum wage has been raised, the number of people who've lost minimum wage jobs and found jobs at below the minimum wage greatly outnumbered those who benefited from the minimum wage increase.

"There's more to this, Julia. Shall I go on?"

"Please do, Justin. I'm learning a lot."

"Okay. Let's say a kid who didn't finish school goes to see a busi-ness owner about a minimum wage job. The kid has never had a job and doesn't speak English all that well. The business owner would like to employ him. But if the owner can't stay in business, he'd have to fire all his workers. The kid will need learning time. He'll need a lot of supervision. Some days he probably won't show up for work, in which case the work would have to be done by other employees, stressing the whole company.

"The business owner likes the kid. He wants to hire him, but he'd lose money if he paid him more than $5 an hour to start. The government won't allow it. He has to pay the kid 15 bucks right off the bat. The business owner is forced to say, 'I'm sorry, pal, I just can't do it.' The kid doesn't get a chance to step on the first rung of the ladder of success.

"Milton Friedman said, 'Minimum wages are the most racist laws on the books.' I don't know whether this is still true or not," says Justin. "Blacks have made a lot of advances because President Trump lowered corporate tax rates and did away with crippling regulations. But there's no question that minimum wage laws work against the interests of people at the lower end of the income scale.

"Black economist Thomas Sowell said, 'The real minimum wage is always zero. This is what inexperienced and low-skilled people receive because of legislation making it illegal for employers to pay them what they're worth.'

"The average person subject to minimum wage is a member of a household that has an income of more than $50,000. I'm talking about the wives of working husbands and young people who are still living with their parents. Surprisingly few people earn their livelihood solely from minimum wages. Minimum wage laws provide little good, but they do a great deal of harm. They should all be repealed.

Julia responds, "All that seems reasonable to me. But minimum wages seem hardly enough to support a family. You talked about millions of people whose wages are even lower than the minimum. Those are certainly not adequate standards of living."

"You're absolutely right, Julia. There are two ways their income could be improved: First, government would have to stop unintentionally making life harder and more expensive for the poor. It sounds weird, but the poor would be helped the most if government stopped trying to help them. Government is funny that way. The actual results are opposite to what our intuitions tell us the results should be.

"Also, literally millions of people work for the government itself. They don't create wealth, but they do consume wealth. Including benefits, they get paid significantly more than people with equivalent jobs in the private sector. Also, without intending to, a lot of these bureaucrats in the long run do more harm than good, which makes it harder for people in the private sector to generate wealth. Millions of Civil Service bureaucrats should be let go.

"If the government were made smaller by several million people, the ones laid off could begin creating wealth themselves in the private sector, instead of making life more difficult for others to do so in government. The cost of government would fall, and the folks who have the most to gain would be the poor."

"How did you get to be so smart, Justin?" asks Julia.

"I'm not all that smart. I'm just open to learning, in a common sense way, about the actual, long-term results of government policies. Some of the smart folks work for government, planning out what the government should do. Those are the bureaucrats and the academics in universities. They don't realize it, but the long-term negative effects of their plans greatly outweigh the short-term benefits.

"Libertarians like me want to minimize the use of force. We want free market capitalism to solve problems. The results are opposite to those of government: The short-term results of free markets are sometimes negative, as when unemployment rises modestly. But the long-term results are very positive. Government should focus primarily on its long-term results."

Zoning

Julia says, "Justin, a while ago, you said that one of the impediments to building new housing is zoning. Tell me more about that."

"Okay, Julia. Zoning is probably the biggest reason why too few multi-family housing developments are being built, causing rents to rise faster than wages.

"Zoning isn't necessary to ensure that factories are not built in residential areas. The people who build factories don't need expensive land for that purpose. The factories themselves are expensive, but they're usually built on out-of-the-way, preferably flat land that's cheap. People who buy houses, however, want them on attractive, more varied land, which is usually costly. Those who develop housing and those who develop industry seldom compete for the same land.

"The first large-scale zoning ordinance was imposed many years ago in Los Angeles. The purpose was to separate industry from residential zones. This would have been done by the free market. But the residents wanted perfection even at the margins, and they wanted government to provide it. Government officials were only too happy to try, because exercising power is their thing. Many voters don't understand that human society is not perfectible and that government should be the last place to try to attain it.

"Anyway, that was just the beginning. Zoning laws have since expanded enormously. Officials now endeavor to set standards of size, dimension, scale, and aesthetic values for buildings and the land surrounding the buildings. They seek to preserve wetlands and desert lands, and they also try to help the poor.

"The ordinances have grown into multi-layered, regulatory boondoggles. Some of them prevent renting a bedroom to a person who's not a relative, as if that's any of the government's business. City planning bureaucrats delay and even ban the construction of housing units, reducing the supply of housing and causing the rents of existing apartments to rise. The people who pay rent are those with lower incomes. Zoning laws hit the poor hardest. Their wages have not kept up with rents.

"When people complain that rents are too high, it doesn't occur to officials to truly solve the problem by getting rid of zoning. This would reduce their power. Instead, they tackle the high rents by imposing rent controls, which increase their power all the more and impose a whole new set of requirements and a whole new set of problems.

"Zoning laws also separate the various functions of cities. A jumble of purposes mixed together in a city seems messy, but it creates social cohesion and makes cities more stable. More people out walking on the streets reduce crime—even more so if they're armed. It's the poor who benefit most from reducing crime. Voluntary human action and people just living their lives with free market capitalism benefits society far more than top-down planning."

Obesity

Julia says, "I'm starting to get heavy, Justin. I hate it, and I can't seem to stop overeating."

Justin responds, "This is a wonderful example of unintended consequences. Almost 50 years ago, Congress passed the U.S. Farm Bill of 1973, which gave American consumers a plentiful supply of food at reasonable prices. Under the bill and its successors, some $20 billion is paid annually to rich farmers who produce staple commodities, especially corn. Harmless, right?

"But the foods produced from these crops—French fries, pastas, pizzas, breads, condiments, sweet deserts, sweet drinks—especially high-fructose corn syrup—are unhealthy. They're loaded with sugar and other carbohydrates, which the body responds to by raising the level of insulin. Insulin in turn signals the body's cells to store fat, and it also generates a craving for even more carbohydrates.

"These subsidized foods are cheaper then healthier foods. The people hurt most are therefore the poor. Even the life expectancy of Americans is now beginning to fall.

"Around the same year, 1973, American obesity began to increase.

More than 40% of Americans can now be classified as obese. The politicians of 1973 couldn't have imagined that their bill would create a dangerous health condition for so many Americans five decades later. Even younger people who are obese are about as susceptible to Covid-19 as those who are over 70.

"If the subsidies to rich farmers were terminated, as they should be, the supply of bad foods would fall, and their prices would rise. The demand for good foods would therefore increase. Suppliers of good foods would compete to meet the demand, and their prices would fall."

"I'll see if I can't knock off those carbohydrates," says Julia. "I'll think of myself as the wife of Tarzan, living in the jungle, eating meat, fat, veggies, and maybe a little fruit."

Healthcare

"Justin, when I walking on the street one morning, I fell and suffered a gash on my arm."

She showed him the scar on her arm.

"Someone called 911. An ambulance took me to the hospital emergency room, where I spent the rest of the day. My health insurance company subsequently notified me that they had paid the hospital $2,000. Do you have any comments about this?"

"I certainly do," responded Justin. "It's a shame you got hurt, Julia, but $2,000 is too much for repairing a gash on the arm. Overall, the cost of American healthcare is about twice too high. The reason is because government is so deeply involved.

"When you go to a doctor, most of the bill is paid by Medicare or an insurance company. Why should anyone care about the costs when someone else is paying?

"This isn't true of most other things. You pay for them, and you darn well know the costs. If one supplier is too expensive, you go to another. If the prices of all the suppliers are too high, you don't buy that item.

"The same thing would happen if you had to pay for your own healthcare costs. You would seek less expensive alternatives. Instead of going to the emergency room, you would probably ask the ambulance to take you to a local clinic, where the cost of patching up your arm would be more like $100, not $2,000. Over time, faced with competition like this, the hospital's costs would fall to keep them from losing business. If you have a cold or other minor medical problem, you might choose to just stay home and not go to a doctor, which you would have done before.

"When I myself first obtained a primary care physician," said Justin, "I told him, 'I consider myself the primary caretaker of my body. You are my knowledgeable assistant. Is this okay with you?' The physician responded, 'It certainly is.' Needless to say, we've gotten along great.

"You would still have a health insurance policy, Julia, although not with the government. Your insurance policy would have a fairly large deductible for the year, say, $2,500. Up to that amount, you'd pay all of your health costs. The insurance company would then cover 100% of the costs over $2,500.

"It would be like fire insurance. You don't buy fire insurance after you've had a fire, as you can now with health insurance that covers existing conditions. The latter isn't insurance; it's welfare. Fire insurance is true insurance. It doesn't cover the costs from the first dollar. The company estimates the chances of a fire. It's aware that you would first pay the deductible, and it sets the premium accordingly, knowing that it would cover the rest.

"If you went to the local clinic, the $100 cost would come out of your deductible—a cost you wouldn't have incurred before. But you're still young, Julia. Chances are, you'd have few medical costs for the rest of the year. The payments made by the insurance company would be mainly for older people who've gone through their deductibles.

All this would cut health insurance premiums, significantly reducing everyone's net costs. Costs would go down even for seniors. The reduction of their premiums would outweigh the amounts they'd have to pay to cover the deductibles.

"You would also have a health *savings* plan to which you would contribute every month. If you don't use all of the year's deductible, the balance would roll over to future years. When you're older and face heavier health costs, the money is there to pay for them before the insurance company needs to start paying. The savings to the system would be enormous.

"When you're sick, Julia, it's your body that does a lot of the healing. Health professionals and prescription drugs certainly assist. But when you have to pay all of your healthcare costs yourself up to the amount of the deductible, you would be sure to use the health professionals judiciously.

"Competition between suppliers would drive costs down significantly. For most people, their healthcare costs would probably not exceed their deductibles. Instead of making payments for everybody's health services all the time, creating mountains of paperwork, the insurance companies would only need to pay the costs that exceed the deductibles. This would be mostly for older people. We're talking about billions of dollars of savings. Health insurance premiums would come way down.

"Associations of hospitals, physicians, medical personnel, and insurance companies lobby Congress to retain the current costly system. They all want to retain an excess of medical personnel. Healthcare is way too costly. The featherbedding should stop.

"Congress should also sharply limit the penalties imposed when medical practitioners lose malpractice lawsuits. When a doctor makes a mistake, his insurance company should pay the cost of repair, of course, but the extra penalty should not amount to millions of dollars, as it sometimes does now, hugely benefiting the tort lawyers. Penalties should be capped at a reasonable amount. This would enable the liability insurance premiums paid by doctors to come way down from their current ridiculous levels, reducing everyone's health costs.

"Insurance companies would also offer a range of policies. Some policies would offer higher coverage with high premiums. Others would offer lower coverage with low premiums. Let's say you wouldn't want to be kept alive with heroic medical measures at the end of your life. You'd rather allow nature to take its course. Bingo, your insurance premiums would fall significantly right from the start, even when you're young.

"If government just stepped away and allowed free market capital-ism to prevail, the quality and availability of healthcare would improve significantly, and its costs would plummet. The people helped most would be the poor."

Lockdowns

Julia says, "Justin, I envy the people who can work from home dur-ing lockdowns. They seem to be sitting pretty. I have to get out of the house to work."

"I don't blame you, Julia. Working remotely works fine for people who are well off. People earning six-figure salaries did very well in 2020. Those making between $50,000 and $100,000 had a drop in income. But people earning under $50,000 were hammered by the lockdowns. Their income dropped, and their health issues have been far more severe than Covid-19 itself has caused. They've suffered declines in their mental health and other difficulties in their personal lives due to the lockdowns."

Victimless Crimes

Julia says, "Justin, I see pictures of cops arresting people for drugs and women for prostitution. You can tell that the ones being arrested aren't rich. It's almost as if the cops are out to get poor folks like me."

"Yes," says Justin. "You can be pretty sure that if upper-class folks were primarily the ones engaged in prostitution and drugs, the laws forbidding those things would be repealed in a hurry.

"When a woman has nothing else to sell, why shouldn't she be allowed to sell her body? A woman who does have other income, but likes the intrigue and maybe just likes sex? She should be allowed to do the same. It's nobody else's business. It certainly shouldn't be the government's business.

"It's true that prostitutes are mistreated, especially at the lower levels, but this is the fault of government for making the profession illegal. Illegal industries attract people who are willing to disobey the law. Those are the people, usually men, who take charge of the women, take considerable money from them, mistreat them, and hold them against their will. If the industry were legalized, the prices would probably fall, and the mistreatment would stop.

"Once legalized, prostitutes could hold their heads high for performing a valuable service. The best ones would probably be widely admired."

Government Welfare

"Lyndon Johnson's Great Society program and its sister program, the War on Poverty, have been in place for more than 50 years. Trillions of dollars have been spent on Medicaid, food stamps, welfare, public housing, rent subsidies, and federal aid to public schools.

"Yet, as you know, Julia, neighborhoods in city centers, mostly under the control of the so-called progressive Democrats, are as poor, crime-ridden, under-educated, and unhealthy as they were when LBJ promised big improvements, if not worse. That so-called Great Society has been a miserable and extraordinarily expensive failure. We should chuck it before America goes over the cliff.

"Black poverty fell by 40% from 1940 to the 1960s, simply because government ended the Jim Crow laws. This meant it ended discrimination by the government and by the courts, the latter of whom had failed to recognize the right of blacks to own property. But after the 1960s, when the Great Society and War on Poverty came in, the advances stopped, and the earned income of the lower classes remained about the same for years. The programs intended to lessen poverty actually prevented conditions from improving.

"Blacks also joined middle-class professions from 1940 to the 1960s at a faster rate than they did after affirmative action programs were implemented in the 1970s. Same thing. Big help, that War on Poverty.[14]

"Under President Obama, racial disparities in income and home ownership widened.

"The *total* income of the lower classes has risen a lot, because of food stamps, Medicaid, children's health insurance, the refunded portion of earned income tax credits, and more than 85 other means-tested federal and state benefits. But those government programs don't raise morale or create self-respect. Income transfer programs have lessened the growth of *earned* income, and probably suppressed it. Plus, they've aroused resentment among those who weren't on welfare, and they've added big time to the national debt.

"The War on Poverty has produced, not a great society, but a failing society. All those income transfer programs should be repealed. All charity should be left to non-governmental agencies and private citizens. They would not only provide needed funds; they would also induce people to take jobs. Here's what I mean: When recipients of

---

14. WSJ, Jason L. Riley, *Progressives Put the Racial 'Equity' Squeeze on Biden. 2/3/21.*

government welfare get a job, the welfare stops. This induces people to remain on welfare, because the extra income earned from the job, over and above the welfare itself, is insufficient to bother with. Private welfare organizations would deal with this issue with greater flexibility."

Anti-Gouging Laws

"Here's another policy that hurts the poor," says Justin. "When a natural disaster occurs, people in the area need supplies pronto, especially food. The best way to relieve the shortages is to allow the prices to rise. This stimulates suppliers to draw products from elsewhere and supply them where the profit potential is greatest.

"Liberals hate that word, profit. They picture dirty businessmen getting rich off of those in need. (Businesswomen, of course, never cause problems. Everybody knows that women are as pure as driven snow.)

"But it's the natural disaster that caused the pain. The business-men are *relieving* the pain. Free market capitalism makes this possible automatically. It creates profit potential where the need is greatest.

"With anti-gouging laws in place, the prices of products most in need are prevented from rising. This removes the profit potential and slows down the relief. Too few of the needed products flow in. The ones that do are likely to go to the stores that have the biggest volume. Needed products don't get to the smaller stores, which tend to be in poor areas.

"No one is responsible for natural disasters. They happen, and they increase costs. The people who live in the area should pay the costs, appealing to private charitable parties for help if needed. Anti-gouging laws slow down the help and hurt the poor the most."

Regulations

"Julia, government regulations are much more costly than people think because the costs are hidden. Regulations just in the year 2018 have been estimated at $1.9 trillion, which is larger than personal and corporate income tax revenues combined. Regulations also block innovation, suppress employment, and devote resources to compliance instead of growth.

"I talked with a man who had once been on the zoning board of a small town. He told me that a fellow had asked the board for permission to set up a hardware store in a part of town that had none. The zoning board turned him down because a woman who lived near where the fellow intended to put the store told them her life would be disrupted by the traffic. She benefited from the store not being built. But the zoning board deprived several thousand people from having convenient access to a hardware store. The number of those beneficiaries couldn't be counted because the store didn't exist.

"Such are the consequences of most government policies. The short-term results are often favorable. But the long-term results are indeterminable and nearly always negative.

"With free markets, the results are opposite: The results are often mildly unfavorable in the short term, but they're dramatically favorable in the long term. The hardware store, for example, would have been built. The woman would have had to accommodate to increased traffic, as the advance of urbanization everywhere requires. And many people would have had convenient access to hardware they needed."

Social Security

"This won't affect you for some time, Julia, but Social Security benefits discriminate against the poor, especially blacks.

"When a person who's receiving Social Security dies, the benefits terminate. The life expectancy of people with low income is shorter than that of people with high income. The life expectancy of blacks is shorter than that of whites. The life expectancy of black men is significantly shorter than that of white women. Therefore, the FICA taxes paid by black men help provide financial support for white women, but not the other way around.

"It would be more equitable if government got out of the deal. All of us should have non-government pension arrangements to which the funds we contribute serve to benefit ourselves and our own beneficiaries.

"Besides, Social Security began in the 1930s when there were about 40 workers for each retiree. Now, there are only 3 workers for each retiree. The program has become Social Insecurity.

"As more baby boomers retire, we're heading for only 2 workers for each retiree. To some extent, the workers are being replaced by robots and other technologies, which of course don't pay FICA taxes and therefore don't help to support the retirees.

"Those two benighted workers won't allow themselves to be taxed high enough to support half the retirement costs of a retiree. Social Security depends on young people supporting the old. Any such system fails when the burden on the young becomes too great. By the time you retire, Julia, Social Security probably won't exist. The FICA taxes you're paying now will have gone up in smoke."

Testing Drugs for Safety

"Here's another issue that's likely to affect you when you're older, Julia. It applies to prescription drugs.

"Drugs are inordinately expensive. A key reason is because government tests drugs for an extremely high level of safety. A strong desire of bureaucrats is to avoid blame. The bureaucrats keep drugs off the market for years, until they're absolutely certain the drugs are safe. The delay causes lives to be lost, because the decedents didn't have access to drugs that might have saved them.

"The standard of reasonableness should instead apply to drug safety. Yes, a few lives might be lost, but many fewer than the lives currently lost because the standard of perfection prevents them from receiving the drugs that might have saved their lives.

"The bureaucrats, however, prefer the current system. They want an absolute minimum of deaths. If a life is lost because a drug proves unsafe, the death can be counted, and the bureaucrat would be blamed. But the lives saved if drugs went on the market sooner can't be counted, and no bureaucrat can get the credit.

"The testing of drugs for safety should be privatized. An array of testing companies would materialize to meet the challenge. Congress should also limit the penalties for drugs that have been found in law-suits to be unsafe. Perfection is too costly.

"One can see the generality here," adds Justin. "With government policies, the benefits are few, but they're obvious. The costs are many, but they're hidden.

"With free market capitalism, the reverse is true: The costs are few, but they're obvious. The benefits are many, but they're hidden."

Testing Drugs for Efficacy

"In addition to safety, the government also tests drugs for efficacy, that is, whether they work better than a placebo or the competition.

Other products are not tested for efficacy. Cars would cost a great deal more if government tested whether each style works better than the competition and the cost of the testing were added to the price of the car. No, the efficacy of cars is properly determined by the buyers. By the same token, the efficacy of drugs should be determined by doctors, nurses, and patients, not by government.

"Julia, there are more ways that government makes life harder and more expensive. They don't affect you directly. They affect everyone, although they may affect you a little more, simply because you spend all of your income on living expenses, whereas people with higher income don't. Are you interested in hearing about them?"

"I certainly am," says Julia. "Fire away."

Federal Flood Insurance

"People want to live near the ocean. The view is no more interesting than a flat field of wheat extending to the horizon. But the majesty, restlessness, and potential danger of the ocean nevertheless has appeal.

"The potential danger is a problem. A person who wants to live near the ocean calls up his representative in Washington and says, 'Mr. Congressman, I want to buy a house on the ocean, and I want you to reduce my property insurance premiums so I can afford it.'

"'Why do you want to live on the ocean?'

"'Because the majesty, restlessness, and potential danger of the ocean appeals to me.'

"'Well, okay.'

"If the congressman gave his real reasons for agreeing, he'd probably say, 'I want to keep getting re-elected to Congress for decades so I can exercise power over others and retire wealthy. I'll provide you with a government property insurance program that has ridiculously low premiums. If your house is destroyed by a hurricane, the cost is covered by the government and mostly added to the national debt. The circumstances of future Americans will be sunny and bright because of the problems we liberals are solving now. They'll be able to repay our debts with no trouble.'

"The congressman arranges for his constituent to participate in a government-owned insurance policy with premiums so low that they don't begin to cover the risks.

"'Thanks, pal,' says the constituent. 'I'll be sure to vote for you, especially if you give me everything else I ask for.'"

Price Controls on Interest Rates

"You didn't ask about this, Julia, because most people aren't aware of the problem. In recent years, the Federal Reserve Bank has kept interest rates unnaturally low. This has not only deprived savers of reasonable returns, it has also widened the gap between rich and poor. With interest rates low, banks are willing to lend to the rich, because they're pretty sure that at least they'll get their money back. But except with credit cards, banks are reluctant to lend to small businesses and common folks because the returns aren't high enough to justify the risks."

Real Estate Markets Could Enrich the Poor

"Here's another cost that's even more deeply hidden, and this one is huge. Most people don't realize that the marketing of automobiles benefits the poor. Here's how:

"New cars cost more than they're worth. The mere fact that they're new adds value to the initial buyers. Used cars cost less than they're worth. As cars move down the income ladder, sales by the rich and purchases by the poor transfer billions of dollars of value from rich to poor. It's a huge private-sector, income-transfer program that happens naturally. No one set it up. What makes it possible is that government doesn't get much involved with automobile markets. It's because auto sales, both high and low, are pretty much free markets.

"Given a chance, the same thing would happen with real estate markets. Prosperous people would overpay to build houses. When they vacate, the less prosperous would underpay to move in. Billions of dollars of value would transfer from rich to poor. This income-transfer program would be much bigger than that which already exists with automobiles.

"But it doesn't happen because almost everywhere you look, government is involved with land sales. Government *owns* a remarkable amount of the nation's land. The production of housing is one of the most regulated industries in the world. Zoning, land use laws, building laws, banking laws, environmental laws, farming laws, mining laws, water laws, and tax laws all interfere with real estate sales. All these laws and regulations benefit the people who work for government, but they prevent a massive income-transfer program that would provide great benefit to the disadvantaged."

The Jones Act

"Finally, the Jones Act of 1920 requires that goods shipped between U.S. ports and territories must be carried on ships built in America, 75% owned and 75% crewed by Americans, with the goods never sold to foreign citizens. These provisions have greatly reduced U.S. shipping.

"Ships built abroad work fine, but they cost much less than those that comply with the Jones Act. Repealing the law and using foreign-made ships would reduce shipping costs and thus cut the costs of products available to Americans.

"The Seafarers International Union, with its 36,000 members, sustains this wretched situation with campaign gifts. America's 328 million citizens are the losers."

"If the Jones Act were repealed, Julia, you'd be able to buy what you need in greater volume and at lower prices. Government's involvement unintentionally makes life harder and more expensive for you."

"Thanks a bunch, Justin. You should run for office."

"Thank you. Unfortunately, I don't have the talent for making large numbers of people excited and happy about public policies. Rush Limbaugh could do it, but he's gone. Donald Trump can do it. He's immeasurably better than the liberals, but he's no libertarian. Anyway, I'm better off writing a book."

CHAPTER 6
Policing America

CRIMINALS ARE THE PROBLEM, NOT THE POLICE

BASED ON PRELIMINARY ESTIMATES, AT least 2,000 more Americans were killed in 2020 than in 2019. Most of those killed in 2020 were black.[15] For every unarmed black American killed by the police, hundreds are killed in neighborhood homicides.[16]

Increases in 2020 murders in specific cities are tragic: Milwaukee 95%, Louisville 78%, Seattle 74%, Minneapolis 72%, New Orleans 62%, and Atlanta 59%. Many children in Chicago were killed.

Conventional wisdom says the killing was due to the economic, civic, and interpersonal stresses caused by the Covid-19 pandemic.

Nonsense. During the first months of the pandemic shutdowns, crime fell globally. After May 25, when George Floyd was killed by a Minneapolis cop, street violence, murder and mayhem surged, but only in America. Very little condemnation of the violence was heard from Democratic leaders. They simply blamed America for systemic racism. There, that was easy.

The cops are scared. If they have to use force on someone who's resisting arrest, they could lose their jobs, their liberty, or both. Better just to respond to calls for service. Contacts between police and civilians have plummeted. Police have stopped enforcing low level,

---

15. WSJ, Heather Mac Donald, *Taking Stock of a Most Violent Year*, 1/25/21.
16. WSJ, Robert L. Woodson, Sr. and Joshua Mitchell, *How the Left Hijacked Civil Rights*, 1/16/21.

quality-of-life laws. Specialized police units that retrieved guns off the streets have been disbanded, supposedly because they were having a disproportionate impact on African-Americans.

Well of course they were having disproportionate impact on African-Americans. That is primarily where guns are being misused. With the police withdrawing, gang members are carrying guns more than ever, and using them.

Law-abiding citizens in black communities are begging for vigorous law enforcement. They know the police aren't the problem. Criminals are.

Government is force. Force is potentially violent. The bigger the government, the more violence permeates society. Including rioting in the streets.

How to Reduce Funding for the Police

For more than 50 years, from 1776 to the 1830s, the United States had no police departments. It was only in the 1880s that all major cities had them. Until then, armed citizens did the policing. The main reason for the switch was because some businesses didn't want to pay the premiums for suitable liability and casualty insurance and preferred to shift the cost to the public. Thanks a lot, guys.

Liberals now have the brilliant idea that if we just cut funding for the police, but don't enable private citizens to do the job, we'll all live happily ever after. What dreams they have! Wouldn't it be nice if they woke up?

Some liberals want to do away with local policing altogether. Their objective is probably to nationalize the police forces of the entire nation.

Did someone say something about the aggregation of power?

Reducing the size of police departments is a great idea, but only if certain conditions are met, as follows:

- Hidden or not, any member of the public can carry weapons without a license. To a considerable extent, the public would police itself, as occurred in the 19th century.

- Police departments may not unionize. Among other benefits of this, bad cops could more easily be fired.

- People can run for election to serve as policemen. This is especially appropriate in the towns and cities where the candidates live.

- The war against drugs is terminated. Drugs are treated as medical problems, not crimes, and information about drugs is taught in the schools.

- Prostitution is legalized. With drugs and prostitution no longer crimes, prices would fall. Bad guys would no longer be attracted to the industries. With nowhere to go, some of the bad guys might learn to become reasonably good guys.

- Businesses that don't have proper insurance against physical loss, theft, and liability cannot obtain financing. Insurance companies would coordinate with banks and finance companies to settle on the proper conditions.

- Cameras at intersections are operated by a consortium of insurers. If the car hasn't stopped when it should have, the car owner would receive a ticket in the mail and a notice from the insurance company that his premiums have been raised.

(A monitor on board the car to detect speeding might elicit similar responses. But this poses technical problems that are much more difficult because appropriate violations would depend on the time of day and the amount of traffic.)

South Dakota permits its citizens to carry weapons without a permit, hidden or not. South Dakota ranks 9th highest in the nation in gun ownership per capita. In firearm homicides, it's only 45th.

New Jersey and Massachusetts, with strict controls on guns, rank last and second to last in gun ownership per capita. But their gun homicide rates are far higher than South Dakota's.[17]

Gun controls are self-defeating. The fewer guns, the more crime.

---

17. AIER, Robert E. Wright, *The Attacks on Kristi Noem Have Only Just Begun*, 1/30/21.

CHAPTER 7
Miscellaneous

SYSTEMIC RACISM IS NONSENSE

UNTIL ABOUT 1960, THE AMERICAN people were racist. They then began an extraordinary moral transformation. Most Americans are no longer racist.

If you ask people what they feel about racism, the answers would not be reliable. But you can determine their true feelings in other ways, as follows:

- If an advertisement makes people uncomfortable, the product doesn't sell, and the ad has to be redesigned. Back in the 1950s, when America really was racist, blacks never advised whites in advertisements how to spend their money. Now, this is common.

- Current TV ads display intermarried couples, sometimes in bed together. Advertisements didn't show this even twenty years ago. Would whites respond positively to such ads if they were racist? Of course not. The ads sell products because neither whites nor blacks object to intermarriage.

- In the 1950s, blacks were not shown in movies as anything but servants. Now, Americans are comfortable seeing movies and TV shows with blacks in leading roles.

- In both of his elections, Barack Obama received a plurality of votes even in states that were predominantly white.

- Before being convicted of sexual perversion, Bill Cosby was considered America's most admired man. Would this approbation have occurred in the 1950s? Not a chance.

The earned income of blacks is lower than that of whites. To some extent, whites are afraid of blacks. Here are the reasons. It's not because of white racism:

- Slavery, which is always accompanied by the ubiquitous use of force, has existed throughout the world for thousands of years. In Africa, slavery and intertribal warfare long prevailed. Violence was part of the cultural traditions that blacks brought to America. With the southern U.S. economy based on slavery, blacks had no opportunity to learn about the rule of law. When they migrated north, blacks brought with them their inclinations toward violence. It's what they knew.

Then came numerous government policies that contributed to the economic failure and violence of blacks, as follows:

- U.S. governments brought on a tremendous increase in welfare. Here's a salient quote from black economist and columnist Thomas Sowell:

  "Black families survived centuries of slavery and a generation of Jim Crow, but disintegrated because of the expansion of the welfare state."

Welfare has caused black families with only the mother as parent to grow from 20% to the current horrifying 67%. The absence of a father in the home predisposes the children, especially boys, to academic failure, criminal behavior, and economic hardship.

- The disastrous War on Drugs: Blacks who supply illegal drugs would be jailed if they went to court to defend their property rights. They have to defend their rights with violence, and they do so mostly in the black communities where they live.

- Low-income housing attracts people who need jobs and repels people who provide them. The isolation makes life harder for the residents. Some of the buildings become slums, which contain an excess of violence.

- From the 1940s to the 1960s, after the Jim Crow laws were reversed, the earned income of blacks increased faster than that of whites. But after the Great Society and War on Poverty programs were imposed, the earned income of blacks leveled off, while that of whites advanced. Those two dreadful programs left black urban areas worse off.

- Now we have liberal "woke" policies, making the police fearful of losing their jobs if they exert force in black areas. Black gang members are therefore using guns more than ever. Rioting, unchecked by the police, has become far more prevalent.

- On several occasions, the Minneapolis Police Union prevented the Police Department from firing Derek Chauvin and other cops after they'd exercised excessive force. In effect, George Floyd was killed by the union.

- Unions hotly oppose charter schools. Unions, which depend on the support of federal laws, help to keep blacks down.

This book describes more than 30 other ways that government policies make life harder and more expensive for the poor.

Taken together, the above factors provide ample reasons why the earned income of blacks is below that of whites. The same factors explain why whites, to a modest extent, feel that blacks are a danger to them. But blacks are a far greater danger to themselves. It's not because of racism; it's because of damaging public policies.

The two most egregious examples of American racism today are (1) the racist attitude of Black Lives Matter toward whites and (2) The belief by most members of the U.S. Congress that blacks can't get along without government help. This implies that blacks are incapable of making it on their own. That's pure racism. Of course blacks can make it on their own. Government just has to stop getting in the way.

CHINA: A GENUINE THREAT

The People's Republic of China poses a genuine threat to America, more serious than the Soviet Union during the Cold War.

For thousands of years, China was the world's leading nation. An extraordinary number of technologies were first developed in China, including printing, papermaking, the compass, gunpowder, printing, the stirrup (which enabled a warrior to fire arrows accurately while riding a fast-moving horse), the blast furnace, exploding cannonballs, sternpost rudders, domestication of the ox, the plow, irrigation, metal bells, wooden coffins, bricks, lacquer, rowing oars, ploughs, production of silk, cultivation of soybeans, wet-field cultivation of millet and rice, acupuncture, paper currencies, hydraulic-powered bellows, bristle toothbrushes, chopsticks, and many more.

China believes that a global order without China on top is a historical aberration. It belongs there. Having fallen behind for some 500 years, the nation is determined to return to its proper place. Beijing intends to become the world's foremost military power, dominating the U.S. and all other nations economically, militarily and technologically.

President Xi Jinping wants to Make China Great Again.

John Ratcliffe, former U.S. director of National Intelligence, labeled China's approach the three Rs: "Rob, Replicate, and Replace." China robs U.S. companies of their intellectual property, replicates it in China, and replaces the U.S. firms in the global marketplace. The U.S. government estimates that China's theft of intellectual property has cost $4,000-$6,000 per U.S. household each year.

China's intelligence services use access to U.S. tech firms to exploit vulnerabilities. Its efforts to dominate 5G technology could increase Beijing's opportunities to collect intelligence, disrupt communications, and threaten user privacy all around the world.

China has gained a dominant position in the mining and world production of rare earths, on which U.S. advanced weaponry, batteries, solar modules, wind turbines, and other technologies depend.[18] Unfortunately, world development and mining of rare earths outside of China is hampered by excessive environmental concerns.[19]

Beijing is working hard to dominate space. The new U.S. Space Force should not simply aid U.S. military forces already operating on land and sea. It should confront China's intention to dominate space around the planet.

China is engaged in a massive influence campaign that includes targeting numerous American leaders, members of Congress, and congressional aides. California Rep. Eric Swalwell (D) is just one of many. President Joe Biden is another.

Individual liberty is not part of Chinese traditions. They believe it is the purpose of the individual to serve the state. They may intend for Americans to serve the Chinese state.

The United Nations projects that, between 2035 and 2040, the proportion of Chinese people older than 65, compared with those of working age, will surpass America's equivalent ratio. This potential

18. National Review, Steve H. Hanke, *China Rattles Its Rare-Earth-Minerals Saber, Again,* 2/25/21.
19. WSJ Editorial, *Rare Truths About China's Rare Earths,* 3/4/21.

Chinese weakness may be why China is hurrying to achieve dominance.

Here's another weakness: China is a dictatorship. In any nation led by a dictator, underlings are reluctant to tell the boss bad news. They fear being blamed, or even killed, for conveying news he doesn't want to hear. The dictator therefore remains unaware of potential problems.

A third weakness: Any nation whose economy is managed from the top down has the same potential problems that are explained in this book concerning the Federal Reserve Bank. In the long run, no economy can be guided well from the top down.

Wait a minute. Castro took power in Cuba over 60 years ago and, and his family remains in control, with top-down management of the economy.

True, but because of the dictatorship, Cuba has become an economic basket case. China is anything but an economic basket case. But how long its dictatorship and top-down economic management will enable it to remain strong is uncertain.

In the meantime, China threatens America. Our leadership should not take it lightly.

Current U.S. leaders don't even want to consider that there are technical means of reducing atmospheric CO2, as explained elsewhere in this book. They're so confident that forcing people to reduce their output of CO2 is the only solution to global warming that they may assume China thinks so too. They may be in for a surprise. China would be unlikely to consider reducing its use of coal, for example, unless the United States looks the other way when China invades Taiwan.

The primary focus of America's national security should be China.

WHAT? REENTER THE PARIS AGREEMENT?

President Biden is arranging for the United States to rejoin the Paris Agreement.

Five years ago, most of the world's nations signed the Paris Agreement, supposedly to reduce greenhouse gas emissions and limit global warming. A few months after his inauguration, President Trump withdrew from the agreement.

The United States has cut its carbon emissions more than virtually any other nation by substantially increasing its production of natural gas, which contains no greenhouse gases.

In 2018, China emitted almost twice as much CO_2 as the U.S. In 2020, China built more than three times as much new coal power capacity as all other countries in the world combined. The Paris Agreement accommodates China with permission to increase its CO_2 emissions until 2030.[20]

The Paris Agreement provides that the developed nations should "take the lead in providing financial assistance to countries that are less endowed and more vulnerable." Third world countries love that sentence. They want to get something for nothing from the good old USA. With Joe or Kamala in power, they likely will.

Complying with the agreement would destroy hundreds of thousands of U.S. jobs.

Few of the participating countries have come close to meeting their CO_2 targets. Yet even if every country met its anti-pollution targets, the changes in the earth's temperature would be almost undetectable.

President Trump's withdrawal from the Paris Agreement was the right move. Reentry is a foolish error.

---

20. WSJ Editorial, *Why Beijing Loves Biden and Paris*, 2/21/21.

How to Discuss Politics

Here's how to discuss politics amicably:

First, suggest the following procedure and obtain agreement that you both will abide by it.

Let the other guy talk first and listen carefully.

Acknowledge what he'd said and express it in your own words.

Obtain agreement that what you said accurately paraphrased what he'd said. You don't need to agree with his statement. But you both need to agree that the way you expressed it properly conveyed his view.

With permission given, then present your view.

Ask the other guy to paraphrase what you'd said. You both need to agree that the way he expressed it properly conveyed your view.

If you both enjoyed the procedure, address another topic in the same manner. Perhaps on another day.

Two Low-Cost Covid Remedies

January 18, 2021. Two effective, low-cost measures that reduce transmission of viruses are in widespread use in other countries:

The BCG Vaccine protects the most vulnerable against tuberculosis. Hundreds of millions of people have taken it for almost a century with few side effects.

A study funded by the National Institutes of Health and published in the journal Cell in October 2020 showed that the BCG vaccine also triggers a general immune response that reduces viral respiratory tract infections by 79% among the elderly. The vaccine also increases the efficacy of other vaccines.

In a trial run in the United Arab Emirates, none of the hospital workers randomly assigned to receive a BCG booster developed Covid-19. But 8.6% of those not given the booster became infected.

UVC Germicidal Lighting, first used against measles in 1937, looks like a bug-zapper, but it zaps viruses and bacteria, not bugs. Studies show that UVC Germicidal Lighting, operating with a good ventilation system, has the same effect as replacing the room's air more than ten times an hour.

These effective, low-cost measures are not widely used in America because they're unprofitable. This isn't the fault of the companies that supply them. Their job is to increase shareholder profits. It's the fault of the U.S. government's heavy involvement in healthcare.

Government should have nothing to do with healthcare. As explained elsewhere in this book, markets free of government involvement would reduce the nation's cost of U.S. healthcare by about half.

Healthcare would also be heavily influenced by people who care—who raise funds to make available the best healthcare for the most people at the lowest cost. Like these two effective remedies, for example.

COVID DEATHS: MA V. FL

May 9, 2021. A Massachusetts friend informed me that Florida had suffered a surge of Covid deaths. She was glad that Massachusetts had not cancelled its lockdown, as had Florida.

Let's see: According to Worldometer, Massachusetts has had 17,682 Covid deaths among a population of 6,893,000. That's .2565%, meaning that a little over one-quarter of one percent of the Massachusetts population has died from Covid.

Florida has had 35,731 Covid deaths among a population of 21,480,000. That comes to .1663%. On a per-capita basis, Florida's death rate has been about 35% lower than the .2565% rate of Massachusetts.

But there's more: People 65 and over are much more likely to die from Covid as those who are younger.

Massachusetts citizens 65 and over constitute 14.0% of the state's population.

Florida citizens 65 and over constitute 20.5% of Florida population—46% higher than that of Massachusetts. Even though Florida's Covid conditions are less favorable, its per-capita death rate was nevertheless lower than that of Massachusetts.

All in all, if Massachusetts had treated Covid in the same relaxed manner as did Florida, I estimate that the number of Massachusetts Covid deaths would have been reduced by at least half.

SINGAPORE MIGRANT WORKERS

December 15, 2020. Singapore had a problem. According to its Ministry of Health, out of 320,000 of the city's migrant workers, almost half, 152,000, had tested positive for Covid-19.

To keep the disease from spreading to Singapore citizens, the migrant workers, mostly from other parts of Asia, were confined to living in close quarters in dormitories, with no air conditioning in the tropical heat. Some lived in converted industrial spaces or walkup apartments. Some lived in the very buildings they were constructing, with portable toilets and miserable sanitation.

Vaithyanathan Raja, from southern India, told the BBC, "Once the lockdown was in place, we were not allowed to come out of the room. We were not allowed to go next door." The BBC reported, "These people were well and truly locked down, with only basic meals delivered to them."

At the peak of the outbreak in April, more than 1,000 new cases a day were detected in the dormitories.

Among the 320,000 migrant workers, guess how many deaths occurred:

Two.

Out of 320,000 people. With only 25 admissions to the ICU.

True, the workers were all of young working age and thus less vulnerable to the disease than older people. And they may have come from areas where people had become immune (although the virus didn't first appear until 2019).

But still, only 2 deaths out of 320,000 people, living in miserable conditions. What lessons can we draw from this?

- Covid-19 is not deadly, especially for those who are neither elderly nor obese.

- Lockdowns are unnecessary.

- Testing is a waste of time and money.

COVID-19 IN TAIWAN

November 16, 2020. The government of Taiwan has imposed fewer controls against Covid-19 than any nation in the world, including Sweden. Except for the month of February 2020, the schools remained open. The government produced daily reports about the coronavirus, concentrating on actual numbers. Some travel was restricted, but lockdowns were very limited. Generally, the Taiwanese have led normal lives.

With a population of almost 24 million, the total number of Covid-19 deaths have been ... get ready for a huge number:

Seven.

Out of almost 24 million people. All of the deceased were in their forties to eighties with preexisting health conditions.

Here's the likely reason for the favorable result: Back in 2003, Taiwan led the world in deaths per capita from the deadly coronavirus SARS-CoV-1. As a result, the antibodies and T-cells of the Taiwanese people were able to defeat Covid-19 because of natural biological adoptability.

AMERICAN OBESITY

Obesity in the United States has become a significant health risk. Federal government subsidies are directly responsible.[21]

Among Americans aged 20 and over, 73.6% are overweight and 42.5% are obese (defined as having a body mass index of over 30). Obesity lessens resistance to infection and is linked to type-2 diabetes, hypertension, and heart disease.

78% of Americans who have been hospitalized or killed by Covid-19 were overweight.

A significant cause of overweight America is the consumption of high-fructose corn syrup in processed foods. The average American consumes about 37 pounds of it in a year, as well as other corn sweeteners.

Sugar is heavily subsidized by the U.S. government. The incentives have created a high-fructose corn-syrup industry that didn't exist prior to the 1970s. In addition, the government in 1973 began paying farmers to grow corn and other agricultural products.

The 1970s were about the time that obesity began to develop in the United States. Funny coincidence, eh?

From 1995 to 2020, corn subsidies in the U.S. totaled $116.6 billion. A good part of this cost was not included in consumer prices. It was absorbed by the federal government and most likely added to the national debt.

The AIER article by Professor Brownstein footnoted for this section quotes portions of a book by Michael Pollan, *The Omnivore's Dilemma*. Some of those quotes I paraphrase in the next four paragraphs:

- Corn is what feeds the steer that becomes the steak. Corn is a compact source of caloric energy. Cows heavily fed on it grow fat quickly, and their flesh marbles well. Corn-fed meat

---

21. AIER, Barry Brownstein, *How Government Subsidizes Obesity*, 4/20/21

contains more saturated fat and less omega-3 fatty acids than the meat of animals that have been fed grass. A growing body of research suggests that many of today's health problems associated with eating beef are actually problems with corn-fed beef.

- Corn feeds chickens, pigs, turkeys, lambs, catfish, tilapia, and even salmon. (Salmon, a carnivore, is now being reengineered to tolerate corn). Indirectly, eggs come from corn. Milk, cheese, and yogurt once came from dairy cows that had grazed on grass. Now they typically come from Holsteins that spend their working lives indoors eating corn.

- A chicken nugget piles corn on corn. The chicken itself was fed on corn. Modified corn starch glues the nugget together. Corn flour in the batter coats it. And corn oil helps to fry it. The leavenings, lecithin, and triglycerides give it a golden coloring, and citric acid keeps the nuggets fresh. These additives can all be derived from corn.

- Since the 1980s, virtually all the sodas and most of the fruit drinks sold in supermarkets have been sweetened with high-fructose corn syrup. After water, corn sweetener is their principal ingredient.

Because of the subsidies, these corn-derived foods are relatively cheap. Americans most affected by the resulting ill-health are those with low income.

FACEMASKS DO MORE HARM THAN GOOD

Regular, everyday facemasks do more harm than good.

Respiratory viruses get into your body by riding on streams of air. The viruses are much smaller than bacteria and can easily slip through the holes in cloth or plastic facemasks.

But most people don't breath *through* the facemasks. The air comes in from around the edges of the masks, carrying viruses with it.

Here's a test: With your facemask on, press two fingers of one hand on the top and bottom of your mouth. With the other hand, press a finger on whichever side of the mouth not covered by the other two fingers. Press all three fingers so that you are unable to obtain air *except* through the mask. Observe that the mask actually moves in and out as you breathe.

Doesn't this procedure make it more difficult to breathe than normal? I bet it does.

Does your mask normally move in and out as you breathe? I bet it does not.

If the above test doesn't feel like your regular facemask breathing, this means your breath does not normally come in through the mask. It comes in from *around* the mask, carrying those pesky viruses.

Many facemasks contain a wire that causes the mask to make a sharp turn around the nose. Good try, but this isn't nearly sufficient to prevent the air from coming in from above the top of the mask.

No good comes from the facemask.

Also, some viruses that came from the sides of the masks adhere to the inside of it, accumulating there, providing an additional source of virus infection.

Even with no viruses present, the air you're breathing from inside the mask is as unhealthy as the air in a room that's poorly ventilated.

Overall, facemasks serve no good, but they do cause harm. Government requirements that you wear them are cock-eyed.

UNIONS: NEFARIOUS PARTNERS OF BIG GOVERNMENT

A multi-year corruption investigation of the United Auto Workers sent two former presidents of the union to prison. A culture of corruption had developed among the leadership, built around kickbacks, embezzlement, and other illicit activities. Hundreds of thousands of dollars of union funds were used to pay for rental villas, golf outings, expensive meals and other expenses for the labor leaders and their associates.

Back in the 1980s, a similar investigation forced the Teamsters to sever its ties with organized crime.

Those transgressions were made possible because unions operate under the umbrella of the National Labor Relations Act (NLRA) and the Taft-Hartley Act, both of which stand behind unions as they currently exist. They should be repealed. Unions are enclaves of wealth not subject to the strictures of free market pricing.

When a union wants to unionize a company, the laws prevent the company from declaring it doesn't want to be unionized. It cannot threaten employees with the loss of their jobs if they vote for the union. It cannot threaten to close the plant if the company becomes unionized. The National Labor Relations Board has the authority to interpret these matters, and they have been prone to come down on the side of labor.

Despite an increasing U.S. population, union membership, fortunately, is declining. In 1983, union members numbered 17.7 million. In 2019, according to the U.S. Bureau of Labor Statistics, union members numbered 14.6 million.

When workers earn more than they would receive if they were not unionized and the quality of work is the same, the products they make have higher prices. Everyone who buys those products pays the higher costs. The poor are the most affected since they spend all of their income to support themselves.

When developed economies shift away from reliance on manufacturing, the line between manager and worker becomes blurred. Computers, automation, and other sources of higher worker productivity result in fewer workers who do the same kind of job. The portion of jobs in the private sector that are unionized has declined from 34.8% in 1954 to only 6.3% today.[22] Public employees, in transportation, utilities, and government, make up about half of all current union members. President John Kennedy's permission for government workers to form unions was a mistake.

Unions create enmity in the workplace. They operate on the assumption that the corporate managers look upon the workers as foes. Unionization creates a we-they feeling among managers, in the sense that the more the workers make, the less that remains for managers, owners and shareholders.

Without unionization, some corporate managers would no doubt react the same way. But most would not. Most managers believe "We're all in this together. I can't get along without you to make stuff, and you can't get along without us to come up with the money, organize the place, and sell the stuff."

Some time ago, I read about a non-union machine tool company that had signed a large sales contract that stressed the company to get the work done. Everyone had to buckle down to long hours. The company's owner set up weekly meetings that all employees were required to attend. He taught them about the company's finances, sales, expenses, depreciation—the works. The explanations came close to revealing what the managers and owner took home. The purpose was to reveal that the workers were being treated fairly and that they were all in it together. The job was completed on time, and the workers were content with their lot. In a union shop, where the union generates enmity between management and workers, any such

22. WSJ, William McGurn, *Joe Biden, 'Union Guy,'* 4/20/21.

explanation would be unlikely.

More recently, I learned of a company in which the owner vetted a potential employee and decided to hire him. "Great," said the new employee, "what do you want me to do?"

"I don't know," said the owner. "Just poke around the place and figure out where you can be the most productive." Unionization is highly unlikely in companies where employees are so empowered.

In 2020, black citizen George Floyd was said to have been strangled to death by a rogue Minneapolis cop, with three other cops looking on. The press erupted with accusations that the cops were racist. The press omitted mentioning that the Minneapolis Chief of Police was black. (The press usually omits news that makes liberalism look bad.)

The press also omitted explaining that on several occasions in the past, those same four cops had been accused of exercising excessive force. The department had wanted them fired. But in every instance, including the George Floyd instance, the Minneapolis Police Union had sprung to their defense, insisting that the errant cops not be fired.

Yes, unions don't want to lose those dues. They need them to pay millions in campaign contributions to liberal members of Congress, encouraging them to continue supporting unionization.

Teacher unions are among the biggest providers of congressional campaign contributions. The unions fight to protect the jobs even of dreadful teachers. The Chicago Board of Education has installed air purifiers in classrooms, conducted ventilation tests, increased cleaning, and developed rapid testing, among other things. It began vaccinating teachers in February 2021. Having been out for months, while still getting paid, the teachers still refuse to return to work.

Unionists often obtain "release time," whereby members continue being paid for their regular job even though they spend full time on union activities. After looking at 150 jurisdictions, the Goldwater Institute documented that more than 400,000 hours of paid release time is granted every year.

The wretched federal laws that give unions their power should be repealed. They help their own members for sure, but they make America poorer.

Employees should be allowed to form an association of workers to deal with management, subject to common or local laws, not federal laws. Most importantly, workers should be able to quit their jobs and find work elsewhere. They should not be locked into a job by a pension arrangement or union rules that require the employee to stay with the company. The employee's finances depend on the company in the present, of course. But the employee's retirement future should not depend on the same company. If it fails, the worker is left holding the bag for the future as well as the present. It's too much risk.

If the number of immigrants is properly limited (which certainly isn't happening now), it would eventually become easier for workers to find work elsewhere if they chose to leave one job and find another.

Americans are having too few children to sustain the population.** This also makes it easier for workers to find another job.

The National Labor Relations Act (NLRA), the Taft-Hartley Act, and other laws and regulations that enable unions should be repealed.

And Americans should have more children.

TIDBITS

America's racial group with the highest income is Asian. Since everybody knows that American whites are systemically racist, they must have allowed the Asians to outdo them by mistake.

** The average woman must have 2.1 children over her lifetime to keep the population from declining. That's called the "fertility rate." In rural, less developed lands, children are assets, and women have many of them to help keep food available and provide for the parents in their old age. In more prosperous nations, children are liabilities. They're costly to birth, raise, and educate, and they impede both parents from having jobs. Throughout the developed world, the fertility rate is lower than 2.1. America's fertility rate is 1.77. Singapore's rate is a rock bottom 0.88.

Toddlers: Congress requires that toddlers riding in cars must be buckled into humongous seats, only two of which fit side by side in the back seat of most cars. Researchers believe that these carseat mandates have induced a significant number of families to stop at two children. This may be partly responsible for the fertility rate of American women being below the rate necessary to sustain the population. Talk about unintended consequences of government policies!

Mr. Biden wants to enable people to sue gun manufacturers and sellers whenever a crime, accident, or suicide occurs with a gun. Way to force gun manufacturers out of business, Joe.

Bill Gates calls for bars and restaurants to be closed for four to six months and for lockdowns to continue much longer. The air Bill Gates breathes is extremely rarified. He's unaware of the hardships small businesses and plain folks are suffering because of the lockdowns down here on earth.

Rare Earth Disaster: In 2010, Congress made it more difficult and expensive to obtain rare earths from the Congo. This has devastated the lives of the African villagers who mine the rare materials. It has also raised the costs of medical devices that incorporate them, including those used to fight Covid-19. Way to go, Congress. You killed two birds with one stone.

Mr. Biden wants to add "racial equity" as a mandate of the Federal Reserve Bank. No central bank can accomplish this. The only position the Fed might take is to increase the amount of freebie money passed out to the public. But this would make inflation more likely. Whoops, inflation would hurt the poor more than the rich. I suggest, Mr. Biden, that you return to the drawing board.

WALTER WILLIAMS QUOTES

The following are quotes from Walter E. Williams, the incomparable teacher and economist, who died on December 1, 2020:

- Nothing in our Constitution suggests that government is a grantor of rights. Instead, government is a protector of rights.

- My definition of social justice: I keep what I earn, and you keep what you earn.

- The better I serve my fellow man, the greater my claim on the goods my fellow man produces. That's the morality of the market.

- Government is about coercion. Limiting government is the single most important instrument for guaranteeing liberty.

- The true test of one's commitment to liberty and private property rights comes when we permit people to be free to do those voluntary things with which we disagree.

- In a free society, government has the responsibility of protecting us from others, but not from ourselves.

- It is government people, not rich people, who have the power to coerce and make our lives miserable.

- Economic planning is nothing more than the forcible superseding of other people's plans by the powerful elite, backed up by the brute force of government.

- Politicians have immense power to do harm to the economy. But they have very little power to do good.

- The public good is promoted best by people pursuing their own private interests.

- Most of the great problems we face are caused by politicians creating solutions to problems they created in the first place.

CHAPTER 8
Liberal Power Grabs

CONTROL IS THE GOAL

NOVEMBER 30, 2020. JOE BIDEN wants to raise tax rates, which will weaken the economy. When they're in power, most liberals consider economic weakness to be immaterial. What they care about is increasing government's dominance. They want a larger share of income to flow to the government. One way to obtain it is to raise tax rates. They're unaware, or perhaps don't care, that raising tax rates slows the economy and in the long run reduces the tax revenues.

The exercise of power is not a means to a favorable goal. The exercise of power *is* the goal. They want the power, and they want control of the money that goes with the power.

Liberals readily hand out charges of racism and bigotry. They neither expect nor want you to disagree. They just want you to obey.

As to Barack Obama, a smart, attractive fellow, the exercise of power is right down his alley. After the credit crisis of 2008, for example, he kept in place most of the conditions that caused the crisis. (See Chapter 1.) He retained the highest corporate tax rates in the world. He imposed numerous regulations that suffocated business production. Most of the regulations were said to defeat global warming. But Obama knew, or chose to avoid knowing, that the net additions to atmospheric CO_2 come largely from coal plants in Asia and that U.S.

regulations would make not a dent in world temperatures. Unable to persuade Congress to impose the regulations, he imposed them anyway by executive orders.

President Obama's most important goal was socialized, single-payer medical insurance. Only once that I know of did he say this publicly while president. Talking to a sympathetic audience of unionists, he said single-payer health insurance was his goal and that all private policies should eventually be pushed aside.

Mr. Obama wants to force socialism on the American people. He wants government to dominate society in every way possible, even though a weak economy may result. This is why he arranged for the most socialist member of the Senate, Kamala Harris, to be president after Biden's senile dementia requires him to leave office.

In 2020, for the first time in history, the government figured it could turn off the economy like a light switch to mitigate a disease.[23] The negative impact of lockdowns disproportionately affect the poor. To Democrats, this doesn't seem to matter.

The New York Times has listed the ten states with the strictest lockdowns: CA, CT, IL, MI, NM, NY, OR, PA, RI, and WA. All have Democratic governors.

According to contact-tracing studies, only 2% of Covid transmissions have come from restaurants. The widespread closings of restaurants and bars, despite having little effect in preventing Covid-19, have had a devastating effect on the 15 million people who work for them, or used to do so. The lockdowns have hit people of low income hard. To Democrats, it's all in a good cause: to impose their requirements on others.

Back in the 1960s and 1970s, Democrats did not insist on having power regardless of consequences. Leading Democrats honestly wanted to do the right things. They did *not* do the right things, actually,

---

23. AIER, Jeffery Tucker, *Many Pathways to Policy Failure*, 1/11/21.

but they were unaware that the hidden hand of government causes more long-term harm than good.

The rejection of Robert Bork for the Supreme Court in 1987 was one dividing line when Democrats went from trying to do the right thing to simply having power. A constitutionalist, Bork believed, as Neil Gorsuch and Amy Barrett do today, that judges should be guided by the language of the laws, not by their own policy predilections. After Ted Kennedy told blatant lies about Bork, his nomination to the Court was rejected.

Another dividing line may have been the scurrilous effort to undermine the approval of Clarence Thomas for the Supreme Court in 1991, with lies about preposterous sexual perversion.

Guess who was chairman of the vital Senate Judiciary Committee presiding over the confirmations of both Robert Bork and Clarence Thomas:

Gentle Joe Biden.

Except possibly for the well-meaning but mistaken Bernie Sanders, current leading Democrats just want the power. They don't seem to care whether their policies work for the people or not. Speaker Pelosi, for example, knew for months that Americans were suffering because of the lockdowns. She had a stimulus bill in her hands, but she delayed it, figuring it would be easier to defeat Trump in the November 2020 election if the voters were suffering.

Many recent college graduates live in a dream world, with their minds full of mush. They want government to take care of all the problems. After they obtain jobs, one hopes they'll balk at the large portion of their earnings siphoned off to pay for it.

In the last three or four years, "woke" politics, referring to concerns for social and racial justice, have consumed the minds of the liberal elite. They seem determined to destroy various private sector institutions and impose larger and more intrusive government. If they succeed, the reduction, if not the destruction, of social and racial justice will result.

Liberals believe themselves to be middle of the road politically. They feel that conservatives and libertarians shouldn't even be considered part of the panoply of political dialogue, because they're evil. All that's left, in their minds, are shades of liberalism. That's why, if you ask a liberal to characterize his views, he or she is likely to say, "I'm middle of the road."

The behavior of prominent Democrats has become bizarre. Ex-Twitter CEO, Dick Costolo, for example, said, "Me-first capitalists who think you can separate society from business are going to be the first people lined up against the wall and shot in the revolution. I'll happily provide video commentary."

Mr. Trump was impeached for inciting an insurrection, which he did not do. Mr. Costolo's incendiary comments above evoked not a word of condemnation from leading Democrats.

The millions of joyful Americans who appeared at Trump rallies prior to the election intended a landslide victory last November. Trump's actual election was prevented by corruption.

In 2022, voters must take advantage of widespread Republican victories in state governments, get rid of the voting corruption, and terminate the Democratic majorities in the House and Senate. They must reject and correct the corruption, especially with respect to the voting machines. They must reject Democratic acquiescence to the liberal mobs whose violence has been underreported by the press. They must reject leaders who are willing to impose suffering on the American people simply to enhance their power.

If these corrective measures fail, American civilization will be headed for the ash heap. We could even be paying obeisance to the leadership in Beijing.

THE TERRIBLE DAMAGE OF LOCKDOWNS

More people will die because of the wretched lockdowns than from Covid-19.

We can only guess how many, because the consequences are long-lasting. Parents have stopped getting their children immunized for diphtheria, whooping cough, and polio, which are far deadlier than Covid-19. People have skipped chemotherapy, because they think Covid is deadlier than cancer, which it most certainly is not. Doctors are already seeing unnecessary deaths from diabetes. The Centers for Disease Control estimate that one in four young adults have seriously considered suicide. Depression, alcoholism, and child abuse have risen significantly. Drug-related deaths have soared. Kids are learning considerably less out of school than they would have learned in school.

Over time, the deaths and negative consequences of the American lockdowns will exceed those of the disease by many times. Lockdowns are especially hard on the poor.

Throughout the height of the pandemic in the spring of 2020, Sweden kept daycare and schools open for all 1.8 million children ages 1-15. There were no masks, no testing, no contact tracing, and no social distancing.

How many Covid-19 deaths occurred among Swedish children?

None, with only a few hospitalizations. Plus, older people living in the same households with children suffered no higher risks.

Countries whose lockdowns were especially severe, like Belgium and the United Kingdom, have suffered among the worst Covid statistics per capita.

The UN has estimated that 130 million people in poor countries will die of starvation because of Covid slowdowns in advanced economies. A study of nine developing countries by the American

Association for the Advancement of Science found that, in the past, skipped meals and reduced portions of food have been fairly common *before* the harvesting of rice in November. In 2020, however, clearly because of the slowdowns, those deficiencies occurred for the first time in April and May, *after* the harvesting, with children affected the most.[24]

The lockdowns were all about saving lives, right?

Lockdowns do not save lives. They postpone immunity. Lockdowns cost lives and decimate the quality of life. People under 70 should mingle and go to work in the natural way. Stadiums should be filled. Without masks, children should attend school, become immunized, and immunize the older folks.

Under these circumstances, Covid-19 would have died months ago, with many fewer Covid deaths and without the personal and economic havoc the lockdowns are causing. The lockdown policies of the liberal elite are so unthinking and so damaging as to be well-nigh criminal.

INDIA'S COVID DEATHS

April 28, 2021. The media is offering scary news about the coronavirus in India. Here are facts:

- According to Worldometer, the total number of Covid deaths in India has been 201,187.

- India's population is 1,366,000,000.

- How many times do the deaths (201,187) "fit," as it were, into India's population number (1,366,000,000)? The answer is 6,790 times. India has suffered 1 death out of 6,790 of its people.

---

24. AIER, Ethan Yang, Lockdowns Have Devastated the Global Poor, 2/10/21.

(To calculate this on a regular-sized calculator, move the decimal points of both numbers six places to the left, dividing 1,366 by .201187. Same answer: 6,790.)

Now for the United States:

- According to Worldometer, the total number of Covid deaths in the U.S. has been 587,384.

- The U.S. population: 328,200,000.

- The U.S. Covid deaths (587,384) fit into the population (328,200,000) 559 times. The U.S. has suffered 1 death out of only 559 of its people.

- 559 is 12.1 times less than the equivalent number for India (6,790). The impact of Covid in the U.S. has been about 12 times worse than that of India.

- Here's another way to think of the matter: U.S. Covid deaths (587,384) have been almost 3 times larger than that of India's deaths (201,165).

- But India's population (1,366,000,000) is more than 4 times larger than that of the U.S. (328,200,000).

- Multiply 3 by 4, and you can see that the impact of Covid on the U.S. population has been about 12 times greater than that of India.

So why is the media making a big deal about India?

Because news of U.S. Covid deaths is old and tiresome. India's Covid deaths, with the April surge, are new and intriguing. Taking advantage of this, the media wants to scare you into continuing to accept the wretched and autocratic lockdowns of U.S. federal and state governments, which have always been unnecessary for everyone under 70. Both the governments and the media want you to bow down and obey.

It's like Lincoln said: "The laws and regulations of the governments, by the governments, and for the governments shall not perish from the earth."

COVID-19 DEATHS ARE EXAGGERATED

November 30, 2020. Using data from the U.S. Centers for Disease Control (CDC), a recent Johns Hopkins study found that the number of U.S. deaths from all causes has averaged about the same over the years, increasing modestly as the population grew.

As one would expect, the study found that Covid-19 deaths reported in 2020 had a substantial spike. But unexpectedly, the number of reported deaths from heart disease, cancer, and other morbidities *declined* in 2020. The declines were significantly greater than those of previous years. They just about matched the 2020 increase in Covid-19 deaths, causing the overall deaths to remain about the same.

The study concluded that the deaths were misclassified. Non-Covid deaths were wrongly reported as Covid deaths.

The Johns Hopkins study was withdrawn, supposedly because it "spread misinformation about the pandemic." Doesn't seem like misinformation to me. The data is readily available. A similar analysis could be done to provide more data and possibly a new conclusion, but no such analysis has appeared.

Not mentioned in the article is a likely reason for the misclassifications: The federal government pays hospitals $13,000 for each Covid-19 admission and $39,000 when a Covid-19 patient goes on a ventilator. This conflict of interest has probably caused the over-reporting of Covid deaths and under-reporting of other deaths.

The impact of Covid-19 has thus been significantly overstated. Many Americans mistakenly believe that Covid death lurks around every corner.

The government probably did not expect its Covid-19 hospital payments to cause the misallocation of Covid death reports. The hidden hand of government usually causes more harm than good, in a manner that is not obvious.

While Covid-19 has not caused an increase in overall deaths, the lockdowns certainly have. Medical procedures postponed, suicides, substance abuse, alcoholism, and education not obtained; all these are up. Mental and physical health is down. The impact of some of these problems will last for years.

IMMUNIZE YOURSELF: GET THE YOUNG ONES OUT

April 6, 2021. People have been scared out of their wits about Covid-19 by the media and the experts,

Worldometer reports that Covid-19 has killed 570,260 Americans. The U.S. population is 328.2 million. 570,260 divided by 328.2 million is 0.174%. This means that 1 person out of 574 people has died from Covid-19 nationwide.

But for young people, the chances of dying are much more favorable. The U.S. Centers for Disease Control and Prevention (CDC) estimated the survival rates for people up to 19 years old at 99.997%. This means 3 out of 100,000 would die.

Only 1 death out of 33,000. Not bad odds, especially since the one who dies is probably obese.

Keeping children out of school and requiring them to wear masks has been absurd.

Healthy young people have virtually no chance of being infected with Covid-19. Get them out and about, with no masks or distancing. Get them to school. They will rev up their T-cells and antibodies and become immunized. Then they can immunize you and everyone else in your household.

AS IF THE LOCKDOWNS WEREN'T ENOUGH[25]

December 21, 2020. Tort lawyers are salivating about class-action lawsuits against businesses for not protecting their workers from the deadly coronavirus. Some 100,000 lawsuits in the next two years could force thousands of nursing homes, hospitals, restaurants, bars, and movie theaters into bankruptcy and wipe out over a million jobs.

According to economist Steven Moore, tort lawyers are "the bottom feeders in the swamp Donald Trump promised to drain."

The Republican Senate passed legislation requiring plaintiffs to prove that the business was *directly* responsible for an illness or death. Speaker Pelosi would have none of that because Democrats love those hefty tort-lawyer campaign contributions.

AMERICAN MYTHS DESTROYED

January 11, 2021. AIER's James Bovard has exposed the destruction of myths that Americans have supposedly held dear:[26]

- The Bill of Rights safeguards our constitutional rights: After the Covid-19 pandemic began, governors in state after state effectively placed scores of millions of citizens under house arrest.

- Our rulers are subject to the rule of law: Not a single governor or mayor has been arrested for violating citizens' rights. Unlike private citizens, government employees have continued to draw full pay even when they weren't required to show up for work.

- Teachers care about students: Despite many studies showing

---

25. Washington Examiner, Stephen Moore, *Trial Lawyers are looking for a $100 billion coronavirus jackpot,* 8/11/20.
26. AIER, James Bovard, *The Year in which Comforting American Myths Were Ravaged,* 12/30/20.

that children are affected hardly at all by Covid-19, teachers have barricaded school doors, just as segregationist governors barred black students in the 1950s.

- Social media and the Internet would provide free information: Reasonable doubts about pandemic policies are suppressed. Wildly inaccurate projections by government's supposed experts are not.

- Average Americans cherish their personal freedom: To Mr. Bovard, this is the saddest myth of all. Most people have submitted to government requirements and the lockdowns "without a fight and usually even without a whimper." The mass fears generated by bureaucrats and politicians have "ripened into hatred of anyone who did not comply with the latest edict."

Liberals are no longer liberal. They no longer support tolerance, open-mindedness, and protection of individual rights and dignity. They've become authoritarian, requiring people to subordinate their individual needs to the needs of society, as defined by the liberals.

It's time for citizens take all this to heart. They may not be willing to confront government, social media, or media authorities standing over them. But they can certainly confront them in the sanctity of voting booths.

THE WRETCHED WAR ON DRUGS

The prohibition of alcohol in the 1920s was bad enough. It increased drunkenness and crime and lowered peoples' respect for the law. But this lasted for only 13 years. The War on Drugs has lasted for half a century and been much more of a disaster.

When any product is criminalized, people willing to risk disobeying the law are attracted to supply it. They raise prices and increase the supply.

Some people become addicted, which is why the righteous public considers drugs to be immoral and makes them illegal. The illegality, which increases the supply, also arouses curiosity and excitement, which increases the demand.

The criminalization of drugs became a losing proposition right from the start. Government was only too pleased to join the fight because it thrives on exercising force. It also loves the money the righteous public is willing to spend on it.

People who supply illegal drugs cannot go to court to defend their property rights against other suppliers because of course they'd be jailed. Instead, they defend their rights with violence or the threat of violence, usually in the homes and on the streets where low-income people live. This violence induces the government to apply opposing force. All in all, the drug laws have been America's biggest source of violence, affecting people with lower income the most.

President Trump claimed that building a border wall would pay for itself by limiting illicit drugs entering the country. Sorry, this does work. Border restrictions increase the cost of transporting drugs. Drug dealers therefore increase the concentrations and the prices. This sustains their profits, but also makes overdosing more likely. After restrictions were imposed on regular cocaine, for example, dealers developed the devastating crack cocaine.

Higher transportation barriers also cause smaller drug dealers to drop out of the market, leaving the better-connected and more violent dealers in charge. This occurred in the 1920s, when Al Capone and other big-time gangsters took over. It occurred again this time when especially violent and resourceful gangsters in Mexico took charge.

America's cost of the drug war has exceeded $1 trillion. The FBI estimates that, in 2018 alone, 1.65 million people were arrested for drugs, disproportionately black and Hispanic. Instead of starting businesses, how many potential black entrepreneurs have ended up stewing in jail, marked for life as convicted felons? Drug laws hurt everyone, but they hurt the poor most. The criminalization of drugs is miserable public policy.

When cops suspect that people leaving a city have made a drug trade, they follow it until the car makes a minor violation, such as a wheel passing over a white line at the edge of the road. The car is stopped and searched. If the cops find a substantial amount of cash, the people in the car are arrested. The police take the cash and sell the car for cash, most of which is used to acquire things the department needs, like military gear to be used against civilian Americans. The people arrested are not prosecuted, because the crime cannot be proved in court.

From 2000 to 2020, some $36 billion was taken in these "civil asset forfeitures." In some years, the amounts have exceeded those of burglaries. In most states, civil asset forfeitures are profit centers for law enforcement. For police departments to gain financial benefits from such arrests is outrageous government overreach.

The War on Drugs has been an utter disaster and should be repealed. If this occurs, a better crowd would be attracted to the industry, and they could defend their property rights in court. Prices would fall, and America's overall violence would be much reduced. The use of drugs would be better dealt with by education and medical care, not jail time. Some of the bad guys might even become reasonably good guys.

A WORD ABOUT GOD

I have no idea what created the universe. I'd give $100 to find out. When I told this to a scientist friend, he said, "I'd put in another $100.

That would double our chances of finding out."

I believe the big bang, 13.9 billion years ago, set in motion a sequence of events that led to the universe as it currently exists.

Mundane things, like rocks and the wind, operate by cause and effect. Living creatures seem to be self-guided, but I believe they too operate by cause and effect.

The human brain has about 100 billion neurons. On average, each one can fire about 200 times a second. And each neuron connects to about 1,000 other neurons. With such complexity, human beings seem to be different. We seem to have been placed here by a higher power. But the sun also seems to revolve around the earth. Both beliefs are homocentric, and I believe both are wrong. Ever since the big bang, no higher power has helped to make living creatures and any of the rest of the universe operate.

I have no idea what came before the big bang. Perhaps our universe, trillions of light years wide, is just a quark in the eyeball of a mouse in a larger universe.

If you believe in God, that's fine with me. But constructing a libertarian society does not require a belief in spiritual matters. A libertarian society simply works better than any other. It's more peaceful, more prosperous, more equitable, and it generates higher morale. It's the best way to bring what the Declaration of Independence calls for: life, liberty, and the pursuit of happiness.

Will this lead to problems? Of course it will. No matter how well organized, human society is never without perceived problems.

Nevertheless, it's time to give the libertarian approach a try. Let's do it before America goes over the cliff and descends into national bankruptcy.

REVERSALS ARE ESSENTIAL

February 5, 2021. The November election was sharply defined:

Republicans loved Trump. Democrats hated Trump.

Democrats, in fact, have become a party of hate.

In the traditions of Woodrow Wilson, FDR, and Lyndon Johnson, liberals have tried to solve social and economic problems with increasing government force. But force causes long-term problems that outweigh the benefits. As economist Thomas Sowell put it, "Today's problems are the result of yesterday's solutions."

Liberals are deeply committed to their solutions. Yet the problems have worsened, making liberalism a source of frustration. The movement seems to attract people who have an excess of personal frustrations. Generally, liberals are less happy, less charitable, and more amenable to violence than conservatives.

Liberals seem to want the executive to be all powerful, and they have confidence that the results will be benign. They fail to recognize that the more power given to the executive, the more people will seek that power to satisfy their own needs. They care less about doing good for others and care more about throwing their weight around. Eventually, those who seek unlimited power want to be bowed down to. The want all the power and all the devotion. These are common characteristics of dictatorships.

When challenged about the rise in the national debt, liberals are inclined to respond, "That doesn't matter. The federal government can always raise taxes to pay for it."

No it can't. The government can raise the tax *rates* on income as high as it likes. But it doesn't control the revenues. Citizens arrange their lives so that they report less income to the government and pay less taxes.

The more stringent the tax enforcement, the more miserable the nation becomes.

Since 1945, federal income tax revenues have hovered around 17% of the GDP no matter what the rates. If the rates are low, the people thrive, and they pay a low percentage of a booming economy. If the rates are high, the people are poor, and they pay a high percentage of a weak economy.

Liberals abhor the Constitution because it limits their power. They consider America to be immoral and feel justified in cheating to attain political power. Having attained power in the corrupt election of 2020, they intend to batten down society with even more force.

Liberals are disinclined to express their views in any detail because they are unable to do so. Other than the stated intentions of a legislation, they have no interest in its actual effects. They choose not to consider, never mind discuss, the long-term results, because those are nearly always damaging. Liberals are therefore discomforted when conservatives express their views. Instead of expressing their own views, liberals endeavor to silence the conservatives, often calling names.

"You want government to be caring, don't you?"

"Yes."

"Good. Anyone who doesn't support the Cares Act is a racist."

But liberals choose not to become aware that the money from the Cares Act was not all that caring and did not stimulate the economy. Its *unstated* purpose was to buy votes and create dependency. Some of the money was used to repay debts. Some of it has enabled people to avoid going back to work. And a great deal of the money is added to the national debt.

"Who cares about the national debt, anyway? That's never caused problems in the past."

Of course it hasn't, because the interest on the debt composed an insignificant portion of government expenses. As the debt has ballooned to historic highs, the Fed has arranged for interest rates to remain at historic lows so that the interest costs have remained a modest portion of total expenses.

But the towering level of debt makes the dynamics all the more precarious. Interest rates will probably rise, possibly by a lot. This becomes all the more likely as citizens realize that higher inflation threatens.

As explained in Chapter 1, the unexpected rise of interest rates to more normal levels would become a burdensome portion of federal expenses. The government might have no alternative but to stop paying its debts, decimating the value of all bank deposits and insurance policies that have invested in federal securities. But at least investment assets other than federal securities would be left with some value.

If the government pursues the worse alternative and creates so many dollars that runaway inflation occurs, however, all assets valued in dollars would become nearly worthless and Americans would be left with practically nothing.

Conditions are in place to create inflation and higher interest rates, as follows:

- Purchasing power has been enhanced by trillions of dollars of freebie Covid payments and giveaways to constituents of the Democratic left. Many people have chosen to not pay their rent or their mortgages because government has eliminated the consequences of not paying. Instead, they've accumulated funds in their bank accounts, ready to be spent.

- President Biden has signed a blizzard of regulations that will impede production. He wants to double the minimum wage, pay over half of unemployed people more than they would make working, and reduce the production of oil and gas.

- Since February 2020, M2 (the measure of the U.S. money supply most commonly used) has grown by an astonishing

$4 trillion—a one-year increase of 26%. This is double the 13.8% growth of M2 during the high inflation era of the 1970s[27] and the largest annual percentage growth since 1943. The same growth looks set for 2021.[28]

There you have it: higher purchasing power, reduction of production, and stupendous growth of the money supply. These are ideal ingredients for higher interest rates and higher inflation.

The problems have accumulated over a long period of time under Democrats and RINO Republicans. But the behavior of the Democrats has become bizarre. If you don't agree with them, they're coming after you and want you to shut your mouth. They blithely add to the gargantuan national debt like there's no tomorrow. To them, it's racist to stop rioters from destroying the center of a city. Liberal unreality and hatefulness are so lacking in common sense that their policies must be reversed.

The nation is closer to bankruptcy than most people know. Corrective measures must be taken, not only in the election of 2022, but also by adopting the only feasible solutions—the recommendations in Chapter 1 of this book.

27. WSJ, Phil Gramm and Mike Solon, *The Risks of Too Much 'Stimulus,'* 2/3/21.
28. WSJ, John Greenwood and Steve H. Hanke, *The Money Boom is Already Here,* 2/21/21.